No Longer Looking for Applause!

...fulfilling your drive for positive recognition, acceptance and approval, permanently!

Rudi Louw

Content

The marvel of the Holy Bible

1. The *theme* and *inspired thought* of Scripture continues *uninterrupted*.

It took *1500 years* to compile the Holy Bible, involving *more than 40 different authors*, <u>yet</u> the theme and inspired thought of Scripture continues *uninterrupted*, from author to author, from beginning till end.

2. *Absence* of mythical stories:

Compare philosophies and theories about creation in the Middle East, Europe, Asia, Africa and Latin America, and you'll find mythical scenarios, gods feuding and cutting up other gods to form the heavens and the earth. In ancient Greek mythology, the Greeks see Atlas carrying the earth on his shoulders. In India, Hindus believe 8 elephants carry the earth on their backs.

But in contrast, Job, the oldest book in the Holy Bible, declares that *God suspends the earth 'on nothing.'* (Job 26:7)

This was said millennia before Isaac Newton discovered the invisible laws of gravity that delicately balance every planet and sun in its individual circuit.

In contrast to every other ancient attempt to give a creation account, *the Holy Bible pictures the creation of the earth in a very scientific manner.*

In Gen 1 for instance, the continents are lifted from the seas, then vegetation is created and later, animal life, all reproducing *'according to its own kind,'* **thus recognising the fixed genetic laws.** Finally we have the creation of man and woman, *all done by God in a dignified and proper manner, without mythological adornments.*

The rest of the Holy Bible follows suite.

The narratives are **true historical documents***, faithfully reflecting society and culture,* **as history and archaeology would discover them thousands of years later. Not only is the Holy Bible historically accurate, it is also reliable when it deals with scientific subjects.**

It was not written as a textbook on history, science, mathematics or medicine, *yet,*

*when its writers touch on these subjects,
they often state facts that scientific
advancement would not reveal or even
consider until thousands of years later.*

While many have doubted the accuracy of
the Holy Bible, time and continued research
have consistently demonstrated that the
Word of God is better informed than its
critics.

3. The Holy Bible is *intact*.

*Of all the ancient works of substantial size, the
Holy Bible against all odds and expectations
survives intact.*

**Compared with other ancient writings, the
Holy Bible has more manuscripts as
evidence to support it than any ten pieces
of classical literature combined!**

The plays of William Shakespeare, for
instance, were written about four hundred
years ago, and written after the invention of the
printing press.

Many of his original words have been lost in
numerous sections, *yet the Holy Bible's
uncanny preservation has weathered
thousands of years of wars, contradictions,
persecutions, fires and invasions.*

*Jewish scribes, **like no other manuscript has ever been preserved**, preserved the Holy Bible's Old Covenant text through centuries. **They kept tabs on every letter, syllable, word and paragraph**.*

*They continued from generation to generation to appoint and train special classes of men within their culture **whose sole duty it was to preserve and transmit these documents <u>with perfect accuracy and fidelity</u>**.*

Who ever bothered to count the letters, syllables, or words of Plato, Aristotle or Seneca for that matter?

When it comes to the New Testament, the actual number of preserved manuscripts is so great that it becomes overwhelming.

There are more than 5,680 Greek manuscripts, more than 10,000 Latin Vulgate and at least 9,300 other versions; there exist a further 25,000 manuscript copies of portions of the New Testament.

No other document of antiquity even begins to approach such numbers. The closest in comparison is Homer's <u>Iliad</u> with only 643 manuscripts. The first complete work of Homer only dates back to the 13th century.

4. In dealing with time, the Holy Bible *accurately foretells what will happen ahead of time, with unmatched results.*

No other ancient work even begins to attempt this.

Other books claim divine inspiration, such as the Koran, the Book of Mormon, and parts of the Veda. *But none of these books contains predictive foretelling.*

This one fact we know for certain, and it is undeniable: *While microscopic scrutiny would show up the imperfections, blemishes and defects of any work of man, <u>it magnifies the beauties and perfection of God</u>, just as every flower displays in accurate detail, the reflection and perfection of beauty, <u>so does the Word of Truth when it is scrutinized</u>.*

Historian, Philip Schaff wrote:

'*...Without money and weapons, Jesus the Christ conquered more millions, than Alexander, Caesar, Mohammed and Napoleon. Without science and learning, He (Jesus the Christ) shed more light on things human and divine than all philosophers and scholars combined. Without the eloquence of schools, He (Jesus the Christ) spoke such words of life as was never spoken before or since and* produced effects, which lie beyond the reach of orator or poet. Without writing a single line, He (Jesus the Christ) set more pens in motion, and furnished themes for more sermons, orations, discussions, learned volumes, works of art, and songs of praise, **than the whole army of great men of ancient and modern times combined.**' (The person of Christ, p33. 1913)

Today, there are literally billions of Bibles in more than 2,000 languages, *isn't it about time you find out what it really has to say?*

Hey listen, the Holy Bible is all about Jesus, the Messiah, the Christ *...and everything about Jesus Christ is really about YOU!!*

Study Tips:

Read 2 Corinthians 5:14, 16, 18, 19, and 21. In the light of these scriptures it should be obvious that if you want to study the Holy Bible *you should study it in the light of mankind's Redemption!*

Daily feed on Redemption Realities, especially Romans 1 through 8, Ephesians, Colossians, Galatians, 1Peter 1, 2Peter 1, James 1, 1 and 2Corinthians, and the book of Acts.

Acknowledgment

I want to acknowledge and thank one of my mentors in the faith, Francois du Toit, for blessing and impacting my life with revelation knowledge.

The portion on *"The marvel of the Holy Bible"* was borrowed from his website: http://www.mirrorword.net/ as students so often feel they have a right to do with things that come from teachers they respect. Just as Galatians 6:6 says: *"Let him who is taught the Word **share in all good things** with him who teaches."*

To all our many other dear friends and our precious family whom we love and to those who helped me with this project,

…but especially to my sweet wife Carmen;

THANK YOU for all your love and support!

Foreword

Thank you for taking the time to read this book.

Let me start off by saying that I am totally addicted to my Daddy's point of reference;

…His love and approval and eternal opinion of me;

I am in love with Jesus Christ, *and that is enough for me!*

The approval of God is so much more than a doctrine, a philosophy, or a theory; it is so much more and goes so much deeper than knowledge; it way surpasses knowledge,

…we are talking heart language here,

Therefore this book was not written to impress intellectuals with knowledge and philosophy, theologians with theories and doctrine, nor English majors with grammar and spelling for that matter,

*…so if you come up with any other definitions, opposing references or find any language inaccuracies in this book, **please don't use it to disqualify Love's own message I bring to you.***

I write **to impact people's hearts**;

...to make them see the mysteries that has been hidden in Father God's heart, concerning Christ Jesus, and really **concerning THEM**, so as to arrest their conscience with it, **that I may introduce them to their original design, and to their true selves;** and *present them to themselves perfect in Christ Jesus* and *set them apart unto Him in love,* as a chaste virgin, *"for by Him all things were created… All things were created through Him and for Him. And He is before all things*

(He has been in existence from the beginning, He has always been in existence, and holds the place of pre-eminence over everything; He is the Prince of LIFE Himself), *and in Him all things consist*

(...everything in creation is still working according to its design and is held together in Him; *in His power proceeding from His heart of love.*

Everything and everyone finds their place of existence; their function and purpose; their place of significance; their very reason for being; *their very home and belonging, in Him who loves them and gave Himself to them)."* Colossians 1:16 & 17

We are involved with the biggest romance of the ages;

…therefore this book cannot be read as you would a novel; casually, because it is not a cleverly devised myth or fable. **It contains revelation and *truth* into some things you may or may not have considered before.**

It is not blasphemy or error. *It is the TRUTH of God, ultimate TRUTH, and therefore has direct bearing upon YOUR life,* the Word and the Spirit is my witness *to the reality of these things!*

I challenge you, be like the people of Berea the apostle Paul ministered to in Acts 17:11. *Open yourself up to study the revelation contained in this book,* but be forewarned, do not become guilty of the sins of the Pharisees, **or you too will miss out on the depth of fulfillment God Himself, who is LOVE, wants to give you**.

(Jesus said of the Pharisees and Sadducees that they strain out every little gnat BUT swallow whole camels. What He meant by that is that *some people **seem** to have it all together when it comes to doctrine, and they love to argue. It makes them feel important, but it is nothing other than EMPTY religious and intellectual pride. They know the Scriptures in and out, and YET they are still so IGNORANT about REAL TRUTH that is only found in LOVE;*

…they are still so indifferent towards the things that MATTERS MOST. They are always arguing over the use of every little jot and tittle

and over the meaning and interpretation of every word of Scripture.

The exact thing they accuse everyone else of doing though; *the precise thing they judge everyone else for,* they are actually doing themselves; that is: **they often completely misinterpret and twist what is being said, making a big deal of insignificant things,** *while obscuring or weakening God's real truth; the truth of His LOVE.*

They are always majoring on minors, <u>because they do not understand the heart of God</u> and *therefore they constantly miss the whole point of the message*.)

Paul himself said it so beautifully:

"…the letter kills but **the Spirit <u>BRINGS LIFE</u>;"**

"<u>knowledge puffs up</u>, but **LOVE <u>EDIFIES</u> (encourages and builds up).**"

I say again: *Allow yourself to get caught up in the revelation I am about to share. Open yourself up to study the insight contained in this book* not only with a desire to gain knowledge, but also with anticipation to hear from Father God yourself; **to encounter Him through His Word, and to embrace truth, *in order to know and believe that God LOVES <u>you</u> and that He has made <u>you</u> ACCEPTED in the Beloved* (in Jesus).**

The whole purpose of you knowing and believing this reality *is for you to get so caught up in it,* **that you too may be totally FREE in your inner-man; no longer desperately needing the approval and acceptance of other people; free from always being influenced and motivated by their acceptance or rejection; no longer bound by their opinions**... **a slave to other people's acceptance or rejection!**

The revelation I bring to you in this book contains within it the voice and call of LOVE Himself to every human being on the face of this earth.

If you take heed to it, it is custom designed and guaranteed to forever alter and enrich your life!

5 *But to him <u>who does not work</u>*
(. . . to him who does not try to make himself acceptable before God by his own works)

But believes on Him, (or trust Him)
(The Greek says: 'But <u>believes in the One</u>,')
Who justifies (even) the ungodly,

his faith is <u>accounted</u> for righteousness

(his faith **is accepted in exchange for** the righteousness he does not possess,
or his faith **is reckoned <u>as</u>** righteousness),

6 Just as David also describes <u>the blessedness</u> of
(So also David **actually pronounces a blessing upon**) the man to whom God (<u>reckons,</u>
or better yet,
to whom God actually **_imputes_**) righteousness
<u>_apart from works:_</u>

7 (He said:) <u>Blessed **are**</u> those
whose (iniquities of the heart
and)
lawless deeds
<u>**are**</u> **forgiven**,

(forgiveness can't be earned it's a
gift)

And whose sins (from the Greek
root 'Hamartano' – missing the
mark ... whose missing the mark,
whose deeds done in ignorance,
confusion, deception, and
spiritual blindness) are covered

(or overlooked, **let go of** ~ see
Acts 17:30)

8 Blessed is the man
to whom the Lord shall not
impute sin,'

(or **against whom** the Lord **will
not reckon** his sin,)

(The Greek actually says:
'Blessed is the man **against whom**
the Lord **shall in no way** charge
his sin)."
                    ~ Romans 4:5-8

Prayer

Father we thank you that You are no longer a God afar off, a God hidden in some heavenly realm beyond our reach, *but You've come to dwell and tabernacle with us.*

We thank you for the living, life-changing, and abiding Word that has come to reside within flesh… within us.

We thank you for its effect upon our lives.

We thank you for its renewing of our minds.

And so as we open the Scriptures, we thank you, o God, *that You reveal truth to us, **and that the grasping and full embrace of this truth secures our liberty in You.***

Thank you Father, for opened hearts, *circumcised hearts.*

We bless You and honor You for Your mighty Word, in Jesus Name.

Amen

Chapter 1

Life more abundantly

In this book I want to bring revelation to you on the Law of Applause, *in order to set you free in your inner man, to such a degree, that you are "No Longer Looking for Applause".*

You see; **Man exists in applause**.

Man's whole existence, Man's whole being is one that hungers for acceptance and positive recognition.

All of mankind finds the meaning for their life in positive recognition.

We cannot exist outside of positive recognition.

Do you realize that?

Can you imagine life, constantly exposed to being ridiculed, being despised, being rejected, being brought low?

How terrible that must be!

I want you to turn with me in your Bible to 1Corinthians 1:4

Now in this epistle to the Corinthians the apostle Paul addresses some very specific problems in the church *as far as the consistency of the behavior of the Christians was concerned.*

But it's interesting to notice how he begins by addressing them *on the basis of what God has accomplished on their behalf*;

...instead of holding before them the error, *he holds before them the truth of what God has deposited within them.*

That was always his focus and emphasis in ministry.

And so there in 1Corinthians 1:4 he says:

*"I give thanks to God always for you **because of the grace of God <u>which was given you</u>** in Christ Jesus"*

As in all my writings, we are going to study *"grace"* together.

Too many of us know grace only in the context of sin, and although grace does deal with sin, and I am about to address it here in this book, *sin is NOT the most accurate context of grace, FAMILY is!*

Grace is not merely God's answer to a sin problem, *but grace more accurately perceived is His expression of sons and daughters.*

26

We were designed and brought forth in grace and established in righteousness *long before sin entered into the world.*

Jesus came full of that original grace and truth, because this was the actual context of Man's appearance in the world.

God's only reference to you is in the context of Jesus,

...who in His very person is the complete and accurate representation of grace and truth!

Listen, I want you to discover the wealth of God's grace as revealed in the New Testament,

...and as you do *you will soon begin to not only see your identity and belonging in Him,*

...*but you will also see with me that* **grace is not God's ability to merely put up with our wrong conduct.**

Grace is not God's ability to just kind of just hold out until some day that maybe we'll eventually change.

But **grace *refers to what God already achieved on our behalf in His Son's death and resurrection <u>to bring about that change</u>*.**

So every time you study the word *"grace," see it in the light of what God has already accomplished **in your favor** through what Jesus Christ did **on your behalf**.

See, the content of grace is always TRUTH, <u>not compromise</u>!

I want to challenge you to never see grace in a religious way of thinking,

'Well, you know, God's grace is just His ability to put up with my sin, turning a blind eye to my shortcomings and just hoping that, in the end, everything is just going to come out right.'

No!

Grace equals GOD'S ETERNAL TRUTH,

...which confronts and challenges all misconduct!

I often say that grace is not like an overdraft facility at the bank, *where you continue to live in the red because of the favor that you enjoy with your bank manager.*

You see, **"life more abundantly" is not defined in terms of survival in the red.**

"Life more abundantly" is *having enough of every good thing* **so that I may always be in a position to bless abundantly in any need.**

Hallelujah!

Read the previous statement again and pay close attention to that definition of grace,

…and let's look at that scripture quickly where I got that definition from, there in 2Corinthians 9.

We'll get back to 1Corinthians 1, but there in 2Corinthians 9 from verse 6 we read:

*"The point is this: He who sows sparingly will also reap sparingly. **He who sows bountifully will also reap bountifully…"***

Would your heart agree to the truth that *God desires a bountiful life for you?*

A bountiful life is God's desire for you, amen!

And then in verse 7 he says:

*"Each one must do as he has made up **in his heart…"***

Here the RSV translation says; *"mind"* but don't let your mind make your decision.

Make your decision in your heart.

Let your heart make up your mind, amen!

2Corinthians 9:7

*"Each one must do **as he has made up his heart**,*

…<u>not reluctantly</u>

…NOR UNDER COMPULSION (some internal or external **pressure**),

*…for God loves a **cheerful** giver* (not only willing, but **freely** willing, with a great attitude, happy to do it)*"*

Here we find then also *the law of applause.*

You see; you can get Man to do just about anything.

Through the law you can motivate him to action every time.

You can motivate him with enough punishment to get him eventually to do something very reluctantly,

*…because he's scared, you see, because he is motivated by **the fear of the punishment** you see,*

Or you can motivate him with a large enough reward,

*…and he'll do it **for selfish gain.***

But in the end all of that is manipulation!

There are no pure motives involved!

…that person's actions are animated or fueled *by the wrong motives.*

The Bible says:

2Corinthians 9:7

*"…God loves **a cheerful giver**…"*

That means **it comes from the heart with no strings attached.**

It is governed **by love alone.**

It is mixed with faith and trust, *but it has no strings attached.* ***It is birthed from love!***

It is motivated by love!

Verse 8 says:

*"And God is able to provide you with **every blessing <u>in abundance</u>**…"*

I like the King James Version there.

It says:

2Corinthians 9:8

*"…God is able to make **<u>all grace</u> ABOUND towards you**…"*

What did we say is *"grace?"*

Grace has everything to do with our original identity; with our sonship.

Grace is everything God did on our behalf in Christ *to restore us and give us our inheritance* as children of God.

Therefore, Grace is God's nature; God's Spirit, God's Truth of who we are and of what is ours in redemption *at work within us, motivating us from within; from the heart.*

It's a faith thing and a love thing.

It's the love and passion of God at work within us!

It's the faith of God at work within us!

It's the power of God towards us who believe, at work within us!

That power then is also at work in our lives and in our circumstances!

It's called the favor and blessing of God at work on our behalf!

That's grace; *that's the definition of it.*

(There are other definitions of grace, *but you won't find a more accurately one elsewhere.*)

2Corinthians 9:8

*"…God is able to make **all grace** (ALL of it) to ABOUND towards you;*

*…**that you**, always having all sufficiency in all things, **may abound to every good work**…"*

*"…God is able to make **all grace ABOUND TOWARDS YOU;***

*…**that you** (from the heart) …**may ABOUND to every good work**…"*

What measures my sufficiency now?

My sufficiency is measured by *the abundance of His grace;*

…**by everything God accomplished on my behalf and released me into in Christ Jesus;**

…**my sufficiency is measured by *the faith impact; the appreciation impact of it upon my heart*.**

Do you see that?

2Corinthians 9:8

*"…**so that YOU** may always have enough of everything and **MAY PROVIDE IN ABUNDANCE for every good work**."*

33

Hallelujah!

Right, so let's go back now to 1Corinthians 1.

Paul says he always thanks God…

1Corinthians 1:4-5,

"…*because of the grace of God <u>which was given you</u> in Christ Jesus*

…*and that <u>in every way</u> you were enriched in Him*

…*<u>with all speech and all knowledge</u>,*"

And then in verse 26 Paul says:

"*For **consider your call brethren**, not many of you were wise according to worldly standards, not many were powerful, not many were of noble birth…*"

Verse 28 says:

"*God chose what is low and despised in the world, even things that are not, **to bring to nothing the things that are**…*"

Why?

Why would God choose **the things that are despised by the world**, *the things that the world would consider as lowly, as loathsome?*

He is very deliberate in rejecting what the world would consider praise worthy,

Why?

Why would God want, *"to bring to nothing the things that are?"*

…because the things that are supposed to be something <u>have measured themselves by wrong standards</u>!

So, their boasting, their confidence, their applause is found in something they think of themselves as,

…<u>but it's outside of their true design; their original design</u>.

God brings that which is low and despised and of no value…

…no one will give them a standing ovation because of their behavior, or attitude, or mentality,

…because of how despised they have become…

…and **He through them *reveals a new law of applause, a new law of recognition, a new law of favor, a new law of acceptance,***

…**independent of their own achievements!**

Do you see, there in that verse 26, do you see those words?

"...worldly standards...noble birth ...powerful ...wise?"

These are things which Man would esteem as GREAT and POPULAR!

...But in Man's most noble act he still stands condemned in his relationship with God.

And so it says there in verse 29:

*"...**so that no human being might boast in the presence of God**"*

Verse 30 (and I prefer the KJV again here, because in this Scripture at least it is more accurate according to the original Greek),

It says:

"Of Him are you in Christ..."

The RSV is also great, it says:

"...He is the source of your life in Christ..."

But I really like this one in the KJV:

"Of <u>HIM</u> are YOU in Christ..."

…because I want us to study together the whole truth of being *"in Christ Jesus"*

2Corinthians 5:17 says,

*"THEREFORE, If **any man** be in Christ…"*

…and don't you get hung up on the *"If"* now,

…the *"THEREFORE"* and the *"If"* refers to a previous conclusion Paul already came to in verse 14, *and it is therefore part of the same conclusion.*

2Corinthians 5:14

*"…**if** (or **SINCE**) One died for all, **therefore all have died**."*

*"…**SINCE** One died for all…**then ALL died**"*

End of argument! Amen?!

*"…**then ALL died**"*

So, whether they've heard of it or not,

…whether they believe it or not,

…as far as God is concerned,

…He has already identified the whole, total, human race in the death of Jesus Christ.

"Of God are you in Christ!"

*"**God has made Him to be our wisdom**."*

*"…**our righteousness, our sanctification, our redemption!***"*

I say again:

GOD has already identified the whole human race in the death of His Son Jesus Christ.

I want you to discover with me *"the law of identification"* called *"the law of faith"* as we consider together our theme in this book: *"the law of applause."*

1Corinthians 1:30 says:

*"**OF HIM** (of His doing) **are YOU in Christ Jesus**,*

*…whom **God** made **our** wisdom,*

*…**our** righteousness, **our** sanctification, **our** redemption"*

That means if **God** made Jesus **my** righteousness,

…it means that **HIS** righteousness becomes **mine**.

If He makes Him to be **my** wisdom, then my own worldly-standard-wisdom **cannot add** to the wisdom HE makes me to be

…it cannot add to HIS wisdom of me and for me, amen!

My own efforts to redeem myself *cannot add to what God has made Christ on my behalf*.

And in the same way my own efforts to sanctify myself *cannot add to the sanctification that* <u>*GOD*</u> *has made me to be in Christ*.

"And therefore…" verse 31 says:

"…as it is written: 'Let him who boasts, boast of the Lord' (not of himself, but *"of the Lord"*)*"*

Chapter 2

More than mere existence

Let's turn to Romans chapter 3 now and let's read from verse 19.

Romans 3:19

*"Now we know that whatever the Law says, it speaks to those who are under the Law, **so that every mouth may be stopped** and the whole world may be held accountable to God"*

Why must every mouth be stopped?

You see; what is it in Man?

*…*I mean, what is it in Man's mouth that must be stopped *if not Man's own attempt and effort to justify himself?*

Man's own effort to justify himself must be stopped.

Man's own effort *through a worldly standard, a standard that this world would approve of,* **to find that standard as adequate for his own effort before God,** must come to nothing, it must be stopped!

You see; Man's whole survival mentality is found and defined in *his effort to so justify himself* that at least *he finds enough reason for being* on this planet.

I mean, **Man in general knows he is born for more than mere existence,**

...the reason for his being on this planet and the reason for him sharing space with other individuals and other parts of creation *is to be found in more than just survival, in more than just mere existing on this planet,*

...breathing air and eating food and hoping to exist for yet another day.

So, Man would immediately involve himself *in defending his own dignity.*

That means Man would immediately begin to explore his environment **to somehow add to his life.**

And he would seek to add to his life *in terms of security and provision for the future,*

...and in terms of dignity and recognition,

...so that in all that Man can achieve he finds a larger platform for his existence,

...So at the end of his days someone could at least raise up some monument on his behalf,

...*even if it is just to be found in the form of a tombstone in a cemetery,*

'...But at least there's more to my life than just a...

...a fleeting moment!

...at least I may preserve some kind of memorial for the future generation of what I have achieved as a man on this planet...'

It reminds me of this old guy trying to justify himself,

...some joke I heard of this old guy whose daughter wanted to get him off of junk food and turned on to health foods...

'Sorry to disappoint you my dear,' he says,

*'I would have tried it if I was younger, but at my age **I need all the preservatives I can get!!!**'*

Ha... ha... ha...

You see somehow there is a drive in Man that always desperately reaches into an undefined future *to justify;*

...to give more weight to his present existence.

And so, **in the course of time <u>a standard is created</u>,**

…**it is called _worldly wisdom_**.

And that _worldly wisdom_ will be the wisdom that is <u>of such a nature that the world approves of its excellence</u>.

What is the origin of worldly wisdom?

I believe it's found in two things:

First of all **Man's own experience,**

Experience would now be Man's tutor.

Man would learn by experience,

…**but his education would be limited to the natural realm of thinking**.

His education would be limited to _sense knowledge_ things.

(That's yet another term with which to become familiar with. I first learned this word _"sense knowledge"_ from E. W. Kenyon. He often refers to this as **a knowledge confined to the realm of the 5 senses (sight, hearing, feeling or touching, taste and smell)**.

(My five senses can touch and learn natural things out of my natural environment,

…_but he speaks of yet another knowledge;_

…_**the knowledge that comes from above,**_

…through the faculty of your spirit,

It is called: *faith-knowledge.*

I am not going to go into all that right now, but if you want to do further study on this subject I suggest you get his book called: *"Two Kinds of Knowledge."*)

But, to get back to my point,

Worldly wisdom is a wisdom <u>that is confined to man's experience</u> as a fallen creature.

We need to understand;

The nature of Adam's fall *brought the whole world under its effect,*

…and its effect was that *a foreign ruler* now dictates over Man,

…so even the good conduct Man dreams of, to become his pattern of life; to become his consistent testimony, *disappoints him again and again,*

…*because of the strong rule of an invisible power* that forces him to do the very thing he disapproves of.

And so, **as a fallen creature, *Man's behavior and Man's education remain limited to the natural realm*.**

In his experience he would find out and soon discover the limits of his own abilities.

Now the second thing that contributes to Man's wisdom is **philosophy and speculation**.

There's another thing in Man that philosophy explores and exploits, and that is Man's ability *to dream about something* that's not real in his experience, **but could *perhaps* still be real**.

So Man, through philosophy would try and add to his experience,

*...***otherwise you see,** *his experience, sense knowledge and scientific information will keep him locked up within a specifically confined and restricted realm of life.*

The scientist would seek to explore and break through the boundaries of what my senses can observe.

So something called the microscope was invented and with that microscopic view he would seek to penetrate beyond the horizon of the senses,

...but he's still restricted to the senses.

Or with his telescope he would seek to penetrate the universe and discover a definition that is larger than his own experience,

…but it still remains limited to life in the senses.

…and so Mr. Philosopher would come along and add his portion,

…he would add his guess, his speculation

…past the frustrated boundary of sense knowledge

So with the philosopher's wisdom added to Man's frustrated experience,

…a standard is formed

It is called,

"*…worldly wisdom*"

Do you see how one generation feels compelled to pass its wisdom; its philosophy of life; its belief-system; its sometimes-frustrated experience; its limited experience and belief-system on to the next generation?

So daddy would tell young Jonny:

'Listen son; let me tell you about life,'

…and daddy would very consciously concentrate *on the positive experience of his life,*

…because he knows there are some rather embarrassing incidents in his past he would want to hide from young Jonny,

…because he wouldn't want Jonny to repeat that

So he would add his philosophy; his belief, to try and add to the quality of instruction and wisdom he gives Jonny.

So, he says:

'Jonny, if you achieve THIS in life, and if you achieve THAT…'

…and usually dad has to tell how poor he was and how rich he became *by the sweat of his own brow, or his own brainpower, his own self-effort…*

…and here we are now really beginning to discover what's at the heart of *the worldly law of applause.*

But I want us to discover that there is *a Godly law of applause,* as well.

I want us to discover *the law of applause,* which can be founded upon three principles.

But I want us to see that **we can really only rely on one of those three principles, *as a sure foundation upon which to build our lives.***

So the law of applause can be founded upon three principles:

- *"The law of works,"*

- *"The law of coincidence,"*

...and the only other principle,

...*the only correct one that gets you anywhere of any real significance <u>as far as life, the way it was meant to be lived, and as far as God is concerned</u>, is* called:

- *"The law of faith."*

In terms of worldly wisdom Man always finds himself confined to the experience and philosophy of the previous generations, or the present generation.

This one problem always persists,

...<u>**Man remains unfulfilled!**</u>

Did you know that even if the whole world stood on their feet loudly applauding you,

...**their applause would be *a mere <u>inconsistent</u>* fulfillment in your life,**

...<u>**a failing fulfillment,**</u>

...**a mere memory of yesterday;**

...there would soon appear within you a new hunger,

...a new motivation,

...a new drive,

...for yet another experience that would exceed yesterday's triumph!

...even though yesterday I managed to gain the whole world, and their approval!

It's never enough!

There is something within me that remains insatiable!

Do you see the frustration of Man's effort?

Chapter 3

The world's standard of approval

I always used to read 1Corinthians 1 and think

'Now why would God go and choose the despised, the low and rejected?

*…shame maybe it's because they've never had an opportunity in life **and He's going to give them their turn now**'*

…but no, listen,

God wants to reveal something to the world.

He wants to expose *the deception* of <u>their</u> standard of approval.

Listen,

The *world's standard* of approval <u>is not</u> *God's standard* of approval.

That's also why the law was introduced;

I'm referring to the Law of Moses now.

The law was introduced to expose to Man the <u>DECEPTION</u>

…of <u>their own</u> standard of approval,

…their <u>false</u> standard of approval

Are you with me still?

I'm referring to Romans chapter 3, verse 19:

"Now we know that whatever the Law says, it speaks to those who are under the Law,"

"…so that every mouth may be stopped"

"…<u>and the whole world may be held accountable to God</u>"

Do you understand verse 19 better now?

Here in verse 19 he is addressing *those who are under the Law.*

The rest of the world, *which is not under the Law,* is already addressed in Romans chapters 1 and 2.

…you can read there from Chapter 1, verse 19 or so, how,

"God did not leave Himself without witness"

…and how,

*"…**their own consciences accuse them**,"*

*"…**or perhaps excuse them**…"*

There is only one of two things Man can do with the dilemma he finds himself in,

…***either he has to feel sorry for himself,***

…<u>***or he has to try and justify himself***</u>.

Man's consistent failure has caused him to settle down,

…either into *despair,*

…or *self-contentment* that says,

'It can never be otherwise.'

…either into despair and say,

'O well, woe am I, I'm just going to just accept… oh …poor little me.'

…or into self-contentment and *self-justification* that says,

'Man I'm not even going to consider that life could be more than I'm enjoying right now…

…so I'm just going to pretend with the best of them and make the best of what I have.'

And so, in Man's excellence, he achieves and he gathers together,

…and it sounds just like that rich man in Luke chapter 12 that Jesus refers to,

…he quickly figures things out for himself, and figures out how the world works,

…and so immediately considers the future of his life *in terms of what he can gather together today*.

And God says of him,

"You're a fool!"

You see, while worldly wisdom would give him applause and say,

'Man, you're so great we're going to make you the mayor of our town,'

…because …I mean,

'…if ever there is a person in our town that we are proud of, that we are…'

'O, we are so glad, sir, Mr. …now what's his name again?'

'O sir, we are so glad that you are part of our community…'

I mean,

'Just look at your large barns… and… and we've heard talks of you planning on building even bigger ones …to secure even a bigger and a better future …for us,'

'O …I mean for you!'

And so the world may praise him,

…but you know what God says about this man?

God says,

"You're a fool!"

I want you to see,

God's measure of wisdom;

…how God measures wisdom,

…and what God calls "wisdom,"

…is not in terms of temporal things,

…but in terms of His original eternal design of our lives!

I want you to see that *sin,*

The word: HAMARTAO in the Greek, *SIN,* simply means:

TO MISS THE MARK

You see **Man could set <u>a mark</u> for himself**

…and he sets his goal,

'This year I'm going to,

…O this year I'm <u>really</u> going to,

…this year, you know, I'm going to,

…I'm going to <u>DOUBLE</u> my income!'

He sets a goal,

…and he tries to reach his mark, *and he goes for it!*

…and he achieves all the applause of his fellow business associates,

…but there's a hunger and an emptiness that leaves him unfulfilled,

…and yet still so <u>deceived</u> at the same time.

You see, we MUST discover **God's** law of applause,

…not the world's standard of approval,

…not some *false* standard of approval,

…some *deception*,

…but **God's *real* <u>standard of approval</u>**!

We must discover <u>the basis</u> of God's approval,

*…if ever we're going to taste **true fulfillment**,*

…if ever we're going to be in a position to communicate the real favor of God to Man!

Our total gospel we live and preach depends upon this discovery!

Our society and almost all of our denominational;

…the whole of our educational system,

*…have been built upon **the law of works!***

We educate our children for at least 12 years,

…and then perhaps another 15 years,

…if one degree is not good enough!

And what do we teach them?

We teach them to excel in life,

…in terms of their own natural skill, talent, and ability,

…to get somewhere!

To get where, really?

'Well …at least my son must have a degree!'

To mean what, really?

'Well …he's got to have some kind of, you know, some kind of security, some kind of guarantee for the future'

You mean …some kind of basis of applause and recognition.

'Yea, that's right …so that when he applies for this or that job at least he's got this letter of recommendation behind him'

To say what, really?

*'…To give further definition to what meets the eye …to give more weight **to his identity?***'

Do you now see what I am trying to say?

…but listen now,

…Say I meet you in the street and you're just Joe so-and-so, that's all right,

…but now, if I hear that you're actually *Doctor* Joe So-and-So, **then immediately I change my attitude towards you**…

Listen to me very carefully now,

*We must stop **drawing our identity from the world we live in!***

…from this natural existence,

…and from worldly wisdom!

…**because it can never define** *our true value and worth,*

…**it only obscures it!**

…*and it causes our appreciation of ourselves and our fellow man to diminish,*

…**which makes the world we live in an even more unforgiving, dangerous place!**

We must stop living *by our natural identity!*

I am not against education and trying to better yourself that way *to provide for your family,*

…but you better put your trust in God!

Either He is the One who gives to all men, life, breath, and all other things, or He is not!

Either He is your real provider, or He is not!

What do you have that did not come from Him in the first place!

There is no security in this life apart from Him!

There is no security in this world!

If there has ever been a generation that is learning these things the hard way it is this present generation!

The world we live in is very unstable, *you don't have to go far to see that,*

…man, just look at the news *and you will soon be forced to agree with me!*

We must stop living *by our natural identity!*

*We must stop **drawing our identity from the world we live in!***

We must discover our true identity in God, it is our only hope!

That identity is of much greater value and worth than anything in the natural we can identify with and try to draw our identity from!

Jesus put it this way,

"Look to the birds of the air, they neither toil, nor gather into barns, (like we in our society have learned to do) **and yet Your Heavenly Father feeds them!***"*

*"…**are you not <u>of much more value</u> than they, o you of little faith!***"*

Can you see how even we in the church have been deceived!

We have allowed *the system of this world,*

…and *the standards of the world,*

…<u>to deceive us</u> *in our appreciation of our fellow Man and of ourselves?*

Because of it we have continued to live in some kind of *disconnect from God's truth;*

…*some kind of disconnect from the reality of God,*

…*and the reality of our true identity; our spirit identity,*

…*in an empty unfulfilled vacuum,*

We keep settling for a lie!

…we keep saying to ourselves and one another,

'*One day we'll arrive,*

…*one day in Heaven,*

…*but not while we're down here on earth!'*

'*Maybe one day we'll get somewhere in the body of Christ, brother,*

… *but not in the here and now!'*

'*Maybe in some other generation,*

…some future generation,

… but not in ours!'

Can you see how we've even taught Christian doctrine *in the same terms as the world?*

'…Maybe one day, off in the distant future somewhere, this old world will be a better place for us all, but not yet, not now, not in this generation; there's still too many things that can't be changed right now… it's going to take a lot of education, and effort, and achievement, building bigger and better, building, building, building, until we finally build a better world for ourselves and for our children!'

Isn't that what we constantly hear… the empty hope of the world… **without substance!**

The religious system doesn't sound any different!

*'…Brother just hang in there, you're not there yet, one day you might get there **if you're diligent enough,** if you get up early enough in the morning …if you pray hard enough, if you read your Bible enough, **if you study hard enough, and apply yourself enough, then maybe one day you'll get there**…'*

Can you see how our whole identity is wrapped up in the Fall of Man?

Can you see how our whole identity is wrapped up in the flesh, *in the natural identity and dimension, in the soul-realm?*

…when, in fact, we are more than mere flesh and blood!

We are spirit beings that just happen to live in flesh bodies,

…but we are more than the flesh body we live in.

We come from above, skillfully designed, and fearfully and wonderfully made.

We were flawlessly put together in our mother's womb.

I am talking about your spirit-man;

…that dimension of you that comes from eternity;

…the real you;

…the one who will never die!

God placed you in your mother's womb,

…and there He clothed you with flesh!

God is spirit, and you are spirit!

You come from above!

You are made in the image and likeness of God, your true Father!

...your Origin!

We are His offspring!

That is where our real identity lies.

This truth of us being the product of His design,

...of His greatest imagination come to life;

...of His love-dream for companionship;

...this idea of us being His offspring and the focus of His love,

...is the greatest truth about us;

...it is the greatest truth about our lives and our existence here on planet earth!

Listen, we need to discover *another law*,

...to operate under and to identify ourselves by and to live by,

... a law that is not bound by time,

...but instead is connected to eternity;

...it is not bound by time, by our performance and achievements and efforts

to try and change or to try and become or to try and get somewhere,

...it is not bound to time; it is connected to eternity!

...to that eternal reality!

...to God's eternal reality!

...we need to discover God's Reality;

...we need to discover God's law of Truth;

...to operate under and to identify ourselves by and to live by,

...it's an eternal law!

It is called,

"...the law...

(...actually it has 3 names in the Bible and is also referred to in many other terms:

- It is called *"the law of faith"* in Romans 3:27.

- It's called *"the law of the spirit"* in Romans 8:2.

- It's also called *"the law of liberty"*

...actually it's called *"the perfect law of liberty"* in James 1:25

And it is also referred to as *"the law of identification or association"* or *"the law of identity"* in Romans 6 and all over the New Testament;

It is *"the in Christ realities"* or *"the in Christ law."*

...but it is all the same law.)

While we are in Romans 3, before we move on, let's just look at the last verse of chapter 2, verse 29, it says:

Romans 2:29

"He is a Jew who is one inwardly, and real circumcision is a matter of the heart, spiritual and not literal. **His praise** (or applause, his approval) *is not from men but from God."*

You see *it's possible* **to even come into a place of religious acceptance,** because of specific conduct that marks my behavior and...

What I mean is:

People want to tag you,

'Are you from the reformed theology background, or the Pentecostal theology

background, or the Baptist background, or Catholic, or perhaps Protestant?

...or are you a Charismatic?

...have you been to Bible Seminary ...which one?

How long have you been in ministry ...and who do you know?

*Are you friends with such-and-such or so-and-so ...**or are you just a nobody?**'*

BUT you see, *and I want you to see this clearly,*

Paul says here in Romans,

...what counts is *God's* approval, GOD'S praise, HIS APPLAUSE, amen!

And so his whole ministry;

Paul's whole ministry was one of *revealing righteousness!*

...the righteousness *of faith!*

...a righteousness that is *of God!*

...*a gift* from God!

...*the very basis of God's approval!*

You are not just an *ordinary* Christian, amen!

There is nothing *ordinary* about you!

When you study righteousness,

...when you study *the righteousness that is of faith,*

...you study the foundation;

THE VERY BASIS of *God's approval of your life!*

Chapter 4

God's standard of approval

What is God's approval of me *related to?*

Is it related to all the suffering and the hardships I've gone through **so that God through my experiences could now purify me?**

Or is it perhaps *related to some kind of achievement that I have achieved under religion,*

…so that perhaps I now feel that my adherence to religion;

…my obedience to religious do's and don'ts *has now somehow earned me approval before God?*

…because, after all, all my efforts and performance, and achievement under religion has paid off,

…it has earned me the approval men!

so perhaps the approval of God is also related to that?

NO!

God's approval is related to <u>what God achieved</u> in His Son's death on man's behalf.

It's called GRACE!

God's approval *is related to GRACE!*

God's approval <u>of my life</u> *is related to what GRACE reveals about me,* amen?!

It's related to eternal truth!

It's related to *God's achievement on man's behalf;*

...God Himself redeeming and reconciling and restoring us back to our original design and place in Him <u>in His Son's death on that cross</u>.

We need to study this **and discover** *what it really means for us!*

*...*so that we can *stand secure* in this knowledge of our redemption and restoration!

*...*and not be swayed through <u>Man's teachings</u>

*...*and <u>Man's opinion</u>,

…because Man's opinion has always been totally polluted with his own experience as a fallen creature,

…and he had to so present himself that at least you don't think badly of him…

In other words his so called standard of worldly wisdom **was always based on lies and deception and on pride,** *blind pride;*

…a self-righteousness full of holes

*…*a pride that is blind and deceived and that has no leg to stand on,

*…*a self-righteousness that misses the mark and falls short!

That, my friend, is the sum total of all Man's worldly wisdom he is relying on for himself,

…and judging you by.

But now let's get back to verse 27 of Romans, chapter 3:

Romans 3:27

*"Then **what becomes of our boasting…**"*

What is *"**boasting**?"*

"Boasting" **is the very nourishment of <u>the soul</u> of Man,**

…and it's the food that Man hungers for,
not Man's spirit, but Man's soul,

…it's the fulfillment of his dreams that
feeds his self-righteous soulish pride!

Once that athlete has so achieved his dreams
there is a platform **for boasting**

…although it's not lasting

…it doesn't matter what level of performance
attained to in athletics _your own inconsistency_
will eventually **disappoint you again,**

…and totally defeat you in the end!

'What is wrong with enjoying sports?'

Nothing!

There is nothing wrong with simply enjoying
sports,

…but you can just watch the golfers to see this
clearly,

I mean, a hole-in-one today, and oops, oh well,
a sixty-three next week;

…and wow one week it's the best and next
week, whew all the balls fly askew and this way
and that way,

…and what a disappointment,

...and you think immediately,

'Oh no man, my life is showing again...'

Why do we think this way?

*...**Because I'm measuring again** you see,*

...I'm measuring,

...because <u>my identity</u>; my pride, is all wrapped up in everything I do,

...I'm seeking desperately <u>to measure the worth of my life</u> in terms of my performance,

...in terms of my achievement,

...in terms of the law of sowing and reaping,

...or in terms of coincidence,

...in terms of luck,

...But I never become satisfied,

I always get disappointed...

...because <u>I do not know who I really am</u>,

...in my pride I think I do, <u>but I don't</u>!

...<u>my estimation</u> of the worth and value of my life <u>remains in flux</u>!

...because I am using the wrong measure to try and measure the approval of my life by!

...and I am miserable and worn out from my own self efforts!

...I remain a slave to the world's false standard of approval,

...the devil's own law of applause,

...and it only produces death in me,

...it produces death in my conscience, and in my confidence,

...death in my relationship with God,

...and death in my relationship with others!

Let's read on,

Romans 3:27-28

"Then what becomes of our boasting?

***It is excluded** (it is done away with).*

On what principle (on what basis can I do away with my blind fleshly pride)?

On the principle of works? **No!**

...but (<u>only</u>) on the principle of faith!"

Only on the basis of faith;

…only by the law of faith *can I do away with the law of works.*

"For we hold that a man IS JUSTIFIED <u>by faith</u> APART FROM WORKS of law"

Paul says:

"For **we <u>hold</u>***…"*

That means it's an ***eternal* truth**, amen!

It is **God's eternal *Truth*,**

God's eternal *plumb line!*

God's Wisdom!

It means **it's important for us *to understand* and *to become persuaded in it,* amen!**

In his argument Paul wanted to convince us that:

*"…man **I<u>S</u>** JUSTIFIED…"*

Hallelujah!

That means,

*"Man **<u>IS JUSTIFIED</u>**,"* amen!

In Christ Jesus Man is justified!

In Christ Jesus, *in His death on that cross,* God justified Man!

So, on that basis

 *"…a man **IS JUSTIFIED**"*

On what basis?

On the basis of Christ's *finished work!*

On the basis of *actually believing it!*

On the basis of *seeing it as reality!*

On the basis of *receiving it!*

On the basis of *fully embracing it!*

See, *you've got to receive that it is so,*

…that in Christ Jesus, *in His death on that cross,* **God Himself justified the human race,**

*…**YOU INCLUDED!***

Verse 28 says:

*"…a man IS JUSTIFIED **by faith**…"*

"…a man IS JUSTIFIED <u>by faith</u> APART FROM WORKS of law…"

*"…a man IS JUSTIFIED …**APART FROM WORKS** of law…"*

*"…a man IS JUSTIFIED …**APART FROM …law**…"*

What law?

The law of *sowing and reaping*,

 …the law of *works*,

 …the law of *Man's own efforts and achievements*,

In other words:

"…a man IS JUSTIFIED …APART FROM

*…**this** law,"*

…*the law of works*,

…*the law of sowing and reaping*,

…*this law of man's own efforts and achievements*

Hallelujah!!!!

We were *JUSTIFIED* **in Christ**, amen!

In His death on that cross, amen!

So therefore,

*"…a man IS JUSTIFIED **by faith**…"* amen!

Because,

"...Man IS JUSTIFIED" **in Christ**, amen!

In His death on that cross, amen!

Romans 3:29

"Or is God the God of Jews only?

Is He not the God of spiritually ignorant Gentile sinners also?

Yes, of Gentiles also,"

Okay, Romans 3 verse 30 now:

"...since God is one (He is God over both the Jews **and the Gentiles**)*;*

...and He will justify,

Or; (*'He justifies and continues to justify'* is a better translation...

It is written in the present continuous tense and *refers to an ongoing law of God, **the law of faith,**)...*

Therefore,

*"...**He justifies the circumcised <u>on the grounds of faith</u>**

*...**and the uncircumcised <u>through faith</u>**"*

78

You see verse 20 through 26 confirms this;

Let's read it carefully, and you will see *I am not just taking a scripture out of context to try and make a point.*

We have already looked at Romans 3 verse 19 that says that,

"the whole world is accountable to God,"

…but now verse 20 continues in saying,

Romans 3:20

"For no human being shall BE JUSTIFIED in His sight BY WORKS of the Law…

Why Not?

"…since (because) through the Law

(This could be the law of conscience and the Law of Moses, *either one,*

…in fact it could be any kind of religious law or moral code,

…*even the standards of your mother and father,*

…*even the standards of your forefathers,*

…*even self-imposed standards,*

...even societal or secular cultural standards <u>that governs the conscience of Man</u>,

you can go study for yourself the things that govern and rule and try to control peoples conscience, *your own included;*

...it all falls under this label of the law of conscience,

...or religious law,

...but in this context he is really making reference to the Law of Moses)

He says,

"...through the Law

(I want you to see that whether you grew up under the Law of Moses, or at least were aware of it and influenced by it to some degree,

...or whether you grew up under Islamic Law or Hinduism,

...or whatever other kind of law that governed or influenced your conscience,

...<u>this scripture applies to you</u>!)

God through Paul says here,

*"…through the Law …**no human being shall BE JUSTIFIED in His sight BY WORKS of the Law**,*

*…since (because) **through the Law <u>ONLY COMES the knowledge of sin</u>***"

The word *"**knowledge**"* used here in the Greek, EPEGNOSKO actually means,

*"…the **full** knowledge"*

Romans 3:20

*"…through the Law **<u>ONLY COMES the full knowledge of sin</u>**."*

(It's the knowledge of sin's full measure, sin's full extent.)

Now let me say something about *the law of conscience* here.

It is a weak law.

You see the law of conscience wasn't enough to live by,

…it wasn't strong enough to reveal sin to its full extent,

Why?

…because I could silence It, I could *lie to myself*,

...I could *deceive myself* easily and *sear my conscience*;

...I could *semi successfully silence it*;

...I could, through pride, get *away with my own efforts to justify myself,*

...so God introduced to Man,

...the Law of Moses!

So the law of conscience gives me a measure of that knowledge of sin,

...and the Law of Moses gives me a stronger measure,

...the full measure,

...it gives me that "full knowledge,"

...the knowledge of <u>sin's full measure,</u>

...<u>sin's full extent!</u>

So the Law *reveals and exposes sin <u>to the fullest,</u>*

...*for what it really leaves me with!*

Because you see, before the Law was given *to challenge my conduct* I could get away with my own prideful efforts *to justify myself,*

…but now the Law puts it in my face and says, *'There it is!'* It says it in black and white; it says it in no uncertain terms, *chiseled in stone!*

And so **the Law becomes a measure to my own efforts to achieve consistent approval before God,**

…and it tells me that I still fall short,

…it tells me that I'm still in need,

…it tells me that I might as well swallow my pride,

…because I will never achieve the approval I so much long for through self-righteousness,

…I will never achieve approval <u>by the law of works</u>,

…I will never achieve approval by any kind of self-imposed law of conscience, or religious law,

…nor even by obedience to this very Law of Moses itself!

That is what the Law of Moses really came to say!

So the Law was given *to stop all boasting in the flesh* …and that's what it was given for.

...the Law was given *to bring to me the full knowledge of Sin,*

...*to show me the full extent of Sin*

...*to bring to me the full understanding of what Sin really leaves me with,*

...*in order to stop all boasting and all reliance on self-righteousness*!

...but it is all that the Law can do!

It only gives me the knowledge of Sin,

...*it cannot set me free,*

...*it doesn't operate in the kind of power I need in order to be free.*

You see, we feel self-righteous when keeping the law we adhere to and submit to and try and live by,

...**whether it is some self-imposed law of conscience or some other religious moral code,**

...*we feel self-righteous when keeping that law,*

...*and condemned when breaking it,*

...*neither situation brings us any closer to consistent lasting true intimacy with God,*

84

...or the approval we desire.

The constant strain of what we are and what we ought to be, <u>only results in an increased sense of distance and separation from God</u>.

It is a *'lose-lose'* situation:

Whether we keep the law we try to live by, or break it, **we don't end up any closer to God.**

Even if the law we try to live by is good in itself.

Even if, like the Law of Moses, that law was given by God Himself,

...it ends up becoming bondage!

Sin's voice of condemnation and the prideful self-righteous voice of the flesh *are the only things that get strengthened by the law,*

*...**even if it is the very Law of God itself!***

It only serves to create an environment, *in which Sin is strengthened,*

*...***and** it hardens Man's heart even further towards God.*

The apostle Paul put it this way:

Romans 7:13

*"But Sin, that it might appear sin, **was producing death in me through what is good,** so that Sin through the commandment of the Law might become exceedingly sinful!"*

(Read Andre Rabe's book called: **Imagine.** *It will really help you grasp these things even better*)

Okay, now that you hopefully understand this thing about the ineffectiveness of law,

…and why God rejects that whole system of self-justification and self-righteousness,

…let's get back to our Scripture.

Let's go to Romans 3 verse 21 now,

*…***and this is supposed to be our focus in our ministry** *because it is God's focus*

Romans 3:21

*"**But** now…"*

Do you have a *"**But now**"* in your Bible?

I've come to appreciate the *"**N-O-W**"* in the Bible perhaps more than any other word.

I want you to know that *the truth of what God has accomplished in Christ is of value for the <u>now</u> of your experience*

Hallelujah!!!

Romans 3:21

"But __now__…"

For too many years *our warped religious thinking* **has kept us in a dream world of anticipating** *having life beyond death…*

"__but__ (we may enjoy having life beyond death) *__now__,"*

*…*__because a death __has__ occurred, amen!__

A death __has occurred__, *on our behalf,*

*…*__and in His death __*we died*__!__

*…*__so you can have life *"__now__!"*__

Romans 3:21

"__But now__ the righteousness of God __has__ been manifested…"

I want you to see as you study this that **there are two kinds of righteousness**.

The one is called *the righteousness of Man* __related to Man's efforts__ **to justify himself, to sell himself;**

*…*__it's related to Man's pride.__

The other one is called *the righteousness of God*,

...or *a righteousness that is of God*,

...which is a righteousness in which God took the initiative,

...a righteousness God totally establishes *through His own conduct*,

...a righteousness based upon a covenant,

...where the second party is not Man,

...but God Himself in the flesh!

Hallelujah!

He entered into covenant with Himself,

...**and we are included** in that covenant,

...**by His doing**!

We are *included* in that covenant;

...*we are benefited by it,*

...**because He has become our legal representative**, amen!

Hallelujah!

All right, now I want us to see something else mentioned here in this scripture*…*

Romans 3:21

*"**But now** the righteousness of God **has been manifested,**

*…**APART** FROM THE LAW*

(…**it's not a part of the Law**),

…although the Law and the prophets bear witness to it"

I want us to see how the Law and the prophets,

…you see, the whole Old Covenant is divided into the Law portion, and the Prophet portion,

So both the Law and the prophet portions under the Old Covenant became a school teacher that pointed towards *righteousness by faith*,

*…***it pointed out to Man the importance and absolute necessity of righteousness *by faith*.**

We can discover this in Galatians, *and we'll get to that in a little bit,* but for now let's get back to our scripture here.

Romans 3:21

*"…the Law and the prophets bear witness to **it**"*

To what?

*"…to **the righteousness of God through faith in Jesus Christ**"*

*"…**for there is no distinction**"*

Why is there no distinction?

Why can there be no distinction to this rule?

Why does it have to be this way?

Why does righteousness only come through faith in Jesus Christ?

Because…

Romans 3 verse 23

*"**since** (because) **ALL** have sinned…*

(Therefore,)

*…**THEY ARE (ALL) JUSTIFIED** by His GRACE **AS A GIFT**,"*

Romans 3 verse 24 says

*"…**through the redemption which is accomplished in Christ Jesus**"*

Chapter 5

What boasting brings us

Let's go back to Romans 3 verse 27 now.

Romans 3:27

*"Then **what becomes of our boasting**?*

Okay, I've said before:

What was our boasting related to?

It was related to *our righteousness,* <u>our</u> achievement,

...*not God's achievement in Christ* but ours, <u>our</u> righteousness;

Do you see that?

So,

*"...**what becomes of our boasting**"*

*...<u>**in the light of this righteousness that is of God**</u>?*

*"...**It is excluded.***

What a disappointment to Man!

…I mean, it means that I could have been the number one scholar finishing first in my high school class, or even in Bible School,

…and all that I've achieved is excluded,

…when it comes to my walk with God; when it comes to enjoying consistent intimacy with God,

…when it comes to my true value and worth in life!

…It means that my noble birth,

…I mean, if I tell you about my pedigree you'll soon find out that in my background there's some big kings and admirals and big wigs, man, I mean these guys made it, there are monuments to them still today

…and there's an association I want to cling to,

…my Family Tree,

…after all, at some point we too were among the Joneses,

…or among the pious,

…or among the humanitarian workers and other do-gooders of this world,

SORRY!

*…*EXCLUDED!

Your boasting is excluded sir!

Romans 3:27

"It is excluded…"

…in the light of that righteousness that is of God!

God has chosen the despised, the rejected,

Why?

Because He wants to reveal to Man the deception of the standard of this world,

…of the righteousness of this world,

…of the achievements of this world,

…of the standard that this world approves of.

Romans 3:27

"It is excluded"

"On what principle?"

The actual Greek says:

"Upon what law?"

Then he mentions two laws here,

*"...On **the law of works?**"*

*"**No,** but on the **law of faith!**"*

Now if you would, go with me to Romans chapter 4 and start reading from verse 1.

Paul writes here about Abraham and he says,

Romans 4:1

"What then shall we say about Abraham, our forefather according to the flesh?"

"For if Abraham was JUSTIFIED BY WORKS, he has something to boast about (before his fellow man maybe), ***but not before God"***

"...he has something to boast about..."

...like even Paul himself had something to boast about *of which he writes in Galatians 1,*

...he says, and I paraphrase,

Galatians 1:14

*"...amongst my own people, I excelled, **I was right out in front, when it came to works...**"*

*"…But **whatever gain I had,**"* he says in Philippians 3:7,

*"I counted it all as loss, **as worthless, in exchange for the knowledge of Christ**"*

*"…**because of the surpassing worth of that knowledge**"*

"…oh, that I may gain Christ and be found in Him"

*"…not having anymore a righteousness of my own, based on law, **but a righteousness based on the faith of Christ;**"*

*"…**a righteousness that is a gift from God;**"*

*"…**a righteousness that is of faith;**"*

*"…**it is based on faith**"*

"…o, that I may know Him and the power of His resurrection…"

…But let's get back to Abraham and what the Scriptures say about him

Romans 4:3

"For what does the Scripture say? (It says) *Abraham **BELIEVED GOD**,*

*…and **THIS** was reckoned to him **AS RIGHTEOUSNESS**."*

And now verse 4 gives us an excellent definition of the law of works, so mark that in your Bible.

Write there in the margin next to Romans 4:4:

'The definition of THE LAW OF WORKS.'

Romans 4:4

*"Now to one who works, **his wages are not reckoned as a gift** but <u>as his due</u>."*

Are you with me?

Let me put it to you in everyday language;

If I work and I'm rewarded *for my labor*, then it's my due, it's owed me, it's due unto me; it's not a gift, *I earned it,* it's my *due.*

So, let me ask you a question.

What is the problem then with the law of works?

Its reward *does not satisfy*.

You see, God didn't just come and say,

'All right, I don't like your laws so I'm just going to kick them over, and I'm going to introduce yet another law and make you live by it; the law of faith.'

No!

That's not what God wants; that's not the way He wants it to be!

God's heart's desire is for the man He designed, *to be a totally fulfilled being*.

God would have to deceive Himself to be satisfied with an unfulfilled creature,

...just like a husband would have to deceive himself to be satisfied with an unfulfilled wife!

Do you see that?

And God knows that within the limits of Man's ability to achieve *through his own conduct, through his own will-power and decision, through some kind of consistency in his own discipline of himself,* **he would soon be frustrated again**.

You know; there is something that the law of works relates to; *it's another law;* it's called *"the law of coincidence."*

The law of coincidence would be Satan's substitute to grace; to unmerited favor.

You go and speak to the fishermen, especially the one in Luke chapter 5,

…I mean, he's been toiling all night, and it's not his first night out on the sea either,

…he's already gained a standard of experience.

His name is Peter,

*…and they're out there, and they're toiling all night, they are working hard, earning their daily bread, **earning some kind of reward.***

When a fisherman starts off he's perhaps the most positive creature on this planet, *because his whole catch already exists in his mind.*

He sees the big one,

'Man, tonight is the big night, I'm going to catch it, tonight boy-oh-boy, we're going to strike it fortunate, we're going to be so lucky, we're going to get the big ones tonight!'

…And he begins to labor within the limits of his own experience, his own skill, his own achievement,

…and the thing that motivates him is yesterday's success

…no, two things, yesterday's success and today's hunger …you see?

…and maybe his little bit of skill and confidence he has acquired over the years.

'At least yesterday I achieved, at least yesterday I got somewhere, and I got some big ones'

…or last month

…or last year

…or last season,

'…and if I can just remember what worked for me then'

…and it keeps him going.

But as the night draws to a close that same man begins to yield himself to another law called *"the law of coincidence"* that operate under the goddess of luck,

'…At least, if my own efforts failed me, and my own wisdom has come to nothing,

…is there not somebody out there, is there not perhaps a god who would just bless me with just one fish?

…oh come on man, please, I don't want to have to go home with nothing…'

And so he's exhausted the energy of his own effort,

…and the wisdom of his own past experience,

…and then he begins to become a candidate for a law of Satan, called *coincidence,*

…the devil's own substitute or alternative for unmerited favor,

…a poor man can become a millionaire overnight if the goddess of luck smiles on him and so works his chances that he wins the sweepstakes.

Many of us have actually been motivated to pray that way…

…as if we're dealing with *"Lady Luck"* when we pray, you know, those one armed banded prayers,

Ha… ha… ha…

'…O God, here's my prayer,'

'…and I once heard that I was supposed to pray just so, according to this principle and that,'

…and so I voice it as religiously as possible, *trying to do everything just right according to my little formula,*

…and phweeeeet there goes,

'…let's hope for the best'

Nothing! He… he… he…

'…And I'm going to just try tomorrow again,'

…and I put my prayer into the slot and hope for the best,

…and phweeeeet there it goes,

…and **nothing** again!

Nothing?

Really?

*'…Somewhere my prayer must have gotten lost between here and there, **or I got the formula wrong***'

…and I try again and again hoping for the best,

…but, **nothing!**

…O, now it is,

*'Yogh, **my right is disregarded by my God!***'

*'**Really God! Come on! Where are You!***'

…and now I have such an inconsistent God that I'm in covenant with,

…He must be sleeping somewhere, maybe He is getting sick of the Rosary and hearing the *"Our Father"*

…or … or,

'I know …maybe He's too busy in India!'

…And I carry on praying,

…and, *'Oh Bro-ther, let me tell you, one day, I tell you, yee-ha! I hit the jackpot today'*

…and it's just miracles and sparks everywhere!

…and, *'I'm in love with Him again'*

…and I rejoice again and I sing,

"God is so good,"

…and I've got a long testimony,

…and, *'He's so wonderful,'*

…and I'm the most positive Christian around!

…but I'm worshiping a foreign God, *a God afar off, a God I don't even know!*

…or worse yet, some other god, some *false god* called *the god of coincidence!*

You know what, that same god of coincidence, *that blesses you today with the sweepstakes or whatever,*

…that same god causes you to be run over by a bus tomorrow,

…no difference,

…same law!

Remember what Jesus asked in Luke 13 when they were talking about the news headlines of the day,

He said to them,

Luke 13:1-5

"…Do you think that these Galileans,

(The ones whose blood Pilate had mingled with their sacrifices – whom Pilate put to death in a gruesome way – *"Do you think that they…"*)

*"…**were worse sinners than all the other Galileans, because they suffered so?**"*

"Or, perhaps those 18 people upon whom the tower in Siloam fell and killed them,"

*"…**do you think that they were worse offenders than all the other people who live in Jerusalem, and that's why they deserved to die in that way?**"*

In other words,

*'Was that the judgment of God; **the fickleness of God,** or what law really operated there?'*

He was challenging their thinking!

'...I mean, judgment had to get them before their time, because they were the worst sinners in town!'

'Or, I know, maybe God's protection just fell short that day!'

But Jesus says,

'**No ways!**'

He says,

'**I tell you, No;** that's not the reason, guys! **It's got nothing to do with that!**'

But you see, the actual point is,

...all of us will likewise perish in one way or another,

...whether it's a criminal that slaughters us,

...or a tower that buries us,

...or a heart that attacks us,

...we will all likewise perish **while we're <u>subject to death</u>**!

Listen, **how do I measure *judgment*?**

How do I measure *God's approval*?

Is it through __fickle__ circumstances that change with the wind?

__What pleases Him__ *consistently?*

I mean, *what __attracts God__ to me?*

My works?

My religious principles and formulas?

Paul says this,

Romans 4:4,

*"To the one who works, **his wages are reckoned __as his due__** and not as a gift."*

Listen, **God is not drawn to me __because of what He somehow owes me__**...

He is not drawn to me __by what I am supposedly due__!

*We can thank God that **He is not attracted to us on that basis!***

His involvement with us *is not based on that!*

If that were the case *we would all suffer His judgment and His wrath!*

So then, **how do I measure God's *approval?***

What pleases God *consistently?*

What would attract Him to me?

Is it my works *or is it simply my faith?*

1John 4:16

*"...we know **and believe** the love God has for us"*

Hallelujah!!!

It's that simple!

Simply believing and knowing** the love God has for **ME!

What pleases God *consistently* **is my FAITH, amen?!**

Not my works, not my religious principles and formulas, *but simply my faith!*

Not my WEAK faith;

...my doubt and confusion, no!

...but simply my BELIEVING;

...simply my FAITH;

*...my TOTAL **faith and trust in** what He says about me and has done for me in Christ*

Jesus to restore righteousness to me - *It's that simple!*

That's what attracts God to me, to draw near to me, to fellowship with me, to do miracles in my life;

…it is simply <u>faith</u>;

…my total conviction and persuasion;

…my agreement with Him!

…my agreement, my AMEN;

…my echo to His TRUTH!

God said it, and God did it,

*…***and He says it still today,**

*…***and I know it and I believe it and I echo my agreement with it,**

*…***and that settles it for me!**

Hey listen, He wants to be free to interact with me **as a gift,**

…and not because **He somehow owes it to me,**

…because **I used the right principle,**

…and applied **the right religious formula,**

…as if intimacy can be earned,

…as if it's my due…

It's a <u>gift</u>, amen!

God doesn't *pay dues,* amen!

He doesn't owe anyone anything, *except maybe judgment, amen!*

It's all a *gift!*

He wants me to simply *take Him at His word!*

His word is His *gift* to me!

That word *inspires faith!*

It's a *gift!*

My faith now *is my gift* back to God!

It's all a *gift!*

God wants to be free to interact with me *on a gift basis;*

…on a back and forth GIFT basis,

…on a mutual love basis,

…and not on any other basis;

...not on the basis of me somehow owing Him something,

...or Him somehow owing me anything!

It's all on a *gift* basis!

That is the only basis of true friendship!

Back and forth gift giving!

*"...we **know and believe** the love God has for us"* - 1John 4:16

Chapter 6

Faith's confidence

"...But whatever gain I had," Paul says in Philippians 3:7-10,

"I counted it all as loss, <u>as worthless</u>*, in exchange for the knowledge of Christ"*

"...oh, that I may know Him"

"...that I may <u>know</u> God the Father,"

"...that I may <u>intimately know</u> Him,"

"...that I may <u>fully know</u> the power and <u>intimate presence</u> of the Holy Spirit"

"...the <u>indwelling Christ</u>"

*"...**and the power** of His resurrection..."*

I've said that **there's no permanent fulfillment in Man's applause,**

...and here in Philippians we discover from Paul that, *in spite of good report,*

"...good repute and ill repute..."

*...there is **a contentment that is unshaken.***

He says,

*"I've learned **the secret of being fulfilled, the secret of being content,** in abundance and in lack,"* - Philippians 4:11-12

*...***that means that lack *can no longer rob me of my contentment in God*...**

*...***Abundance *can no longer encourage me in my contentment*...**

*...***can no longer *add to my <u>life</u>***

*...***can no longer *add to my fulfillment* in God!**

Do you see that?

Listen, we want to discover **the basis, the foundation, *the substance* of the law of faith***...*

*...***it's larger than anything that you can measure *in terms of temporal value.***

Hallelujah!

Let's quickly go to Philippians chapter 3.

I just want us to have a glimpse at Paul's pedigree.

You see Paul discovered the principle that **Christianity is not educating the best Paul or the best Rudi or the best of YOU**

*…*so here in Philippians chapter 3, verse 3, he writes this,

"For we are the true circumcision who worship God in spirit and glory (or boast) *in Christ Jesus* (and not in our own effort) ***and put no confidence in the flesh****"*

Then verse 4 he says

*"For though I myself **have reason for confidence in the flesh** also…"*

Boy, Paul was quite a man, wasn't he?

Remember in chapter 1 of 1Corinthians in verse 26 he says, and I paraphrase,

*"For consider your call, brethren; **not many of you** were **of noble birth** and **wise according to worldly standards,** and **mighty in influence;** and **mighty successful men** and so on and so forth,"*

*"…some of you were, **but not many**…"*

But now here in Philippians he speaks of himself and he says that *he actually was one of those.*

He says, and I paraphrase,

"Listen, if you want to measure me in the flesh, have you considered that I do have something to say about myself,"

He says,

"Let me boast a little bit about my pedigree."

He says,

*"If any other man thinks he has reason for confidence in the flesh **I have more**."*

Ha... ha... ha...

Boy-oh-boy, you're quite the guy, hey Paul?

He says, and again I paraphrase,

"Listen man, I was circumcised on the eighth day, I am of the people of Israel, God's chosen people, and on top of that, I am of the tribe of Benjamin, highly favored, man I tell you, I am a Hebrew born of Hebrews, I'm not mixed with any other race and therefore considered impure by the Jews, man I'm a Hebrew of Hebrews, even among the Hebrews I stand out;"

"...and if you need to further know, listen man, as far as the Law of Moses is concerned, I am as devoted as you can get; a Pharisee, that means I knew every religious principle and formula by heart and I followed them all consistently;"

"…as far as my zeal is concerned I don't think any of you can beat me; I became known as 'persecutor of the church,' and I was proud of it, all my fellow religious leaders praised me, man I even thought that God was pleased with my conduct,"

"…so as far as works and performance and religious achievement, none of you can outdo me!!"

…You see *he had everything going for him,* man, in terms of *noble birth,* and in terms of *the people he was associated with,* in terms of *his religious knowledge and experience,* in terms of *zeal,* in terms of *excellence* in his natural man *he had everything to boast in…*

He says,

Philippians 3:6

"… when it comes to the righteousness of works; my own righteousness under the Law, what else can I say, blameless, man, BLAMELESS!!"

You see that's another kind of righteousness he's talking about,

"…righteousness under the Law."

What does *"righteousness under the Law"* base itself upon; *what does it rely on?*

Man's *achievement.*

Do you see that with me?

"Righteousness under the Law;" religious righteousness …is nothing other than **my own pride,** *my own righteousness,* **my own** *performance* **under the Law, my own achievement under religion.**

It is the righteousness of works and it is something totally different from the *righteousness of faith.*

***It is inferior to* the righteousness of** *faith.*

It is inferior to faith!

Just look at it, Paul says,

Philippians 3:6

"…as far as righteousness under the Law is concerned, blameless! Man, I got 10 out of 10!"

…**But he wasn't that consistent though,**

…**because in chapter 7 of Romans,** *Paul becomes real honest about his performance and achievement under the Law,*

…**about his** *"righteousness under the Law;"*

…**this** *"righteousness of works"*

116

…He speaks about the fact that, **even though his blameless conduct could fool his fellow Pharisees,**

…he couldn't quite fool himself…

You see **he knew that inside of himself** *he was empty and unfulfilled…*

…He was so empty

…He was filled with insatiable cravings of all sorts…

…**He knew that** *inside of himself he was a wretched, miserable man…*

…**for the very things the Law instructed him in, was consistently the things he failed to do in private,**

…in his heart and in his attitude…

…especially in terms of the standard that Jesus sets when He says,

Matthew 5:22

*"Listen, never mind murdering your brother, **if you resent him in your heart you've already killed him***"

He says,

Matthew 5:27

"Never mind adultery, in terms of the act of adultery,"

He says,

"If you even just look at a woman with your eyes and begin to lust after her you've already committed adultery..."

And so, if Paul measures his righteousness in terms of the Law, **in terms of Man's opinion**, he could say that,

Philippians 3:6

"...according to the Law I've lived a blameless life..."

You see anything that he could add to his life **in the eyes of men**,

...anything that could bolster his pride in front of others, *as far as what Man considers to be excellence in life and ministry*, was already there...

'...But in spite of it, I know that I am empty and unfulfilled;

...I know, that before God, I am failing miserably,

...I am filled with all manner of evil,

…it's not just these lousy attitudes against my fellow Man that are consuming me,

…but I am also filled with all manner of insatiable cravings I am not supposed to have,'

'I know, that inside myself, I am miserable, a wretched man,'

'…so what if I've impressed Man?'

'…I am still lacking!'

'…there is something else I am missing when I measure myself against the standard of the Law, what is it?'

'What more do I need?'

If his religious pride *was not enough;*

…if his own self-righteousness *was not enough,* **what more did he need?**

Let's read on here in Philippians chapter 3:7,

"But **whatever <u>gain</u> I had"**

What was the measure of Paul's gain?

It was his *spiritual pride;*

…his supposed superior *religious righteousness;*

119

*…*his own *achievement;*

*…*the righteousness of *works by which he could impress men.*

And now he says,

Philippians 3:7

"*…whatever <u>gain</u> I had*"

'*…God is going to use it for His kingdom!'*

He… He… He…

NO!

"*…Whatever I achieved **through my own intellect and effort,** you know,*"

'*…God is going to use it for His glory, you know,'*

'*…as far as the character that He has formed in my life through it'*

Deception!

What character?

*He certainly wasn't involved in forming **what you call <u>character</u>,** Mister!*

Hey listen,

God is not to blame for the kind of character <u>worldly wisdom and your own deception and manipulation of others formed in you</u>,

...that is not character!

If it is not love forming your character,

...if what you call character is not formed by love,

...it's nothing but EMPTY PRIDE!

God is not to blame for that kind of EMPTY character!

Religious achievement is!

Worldly wisdom and pride is!

Paul says,

"...whatever <u>gain</u> I had,"

I want you to see and know and understand *fully* that *that gain Paul is talking about was an EMPTY gain;*

...<u>it was no real gain at all</u>!

*...o, it might have *appeared* as gain,*

...but <u>it was missing the mark</u>!

...that gain was within the scope and the measure of worldly wisdom,

...and *it was missing the mark!*

You see the new creation *is not something God <u>adds to</u> the old creation!*

The new creation is new, *brand new,*

...<u>*a brand new mindset and identity*</u>!

Hallelujah!

...it's not God, *patching up the old garment,*

...God, through various circumstances, *refining and shaping my old rotten character <u>some more</u>*...

...I'm telling you, if that's the case,

...*God, patching up the old garment,*

...*just trying to improve it a little*...

Jesus says,

"A worse tear will come, and more nakedness will be the result." - Mark 2:21

Nothing of your old self,

...*of your supposed developed wisdom and character <u>is worth adding to</u>!*

122

Nothing of your old identity,

...is worth preserving!

He has given us *new* robes of righteousness,

...<u>a new identity</u> in Him,

...<u>a new mindset</u>,

...and a new attitude and actions come with it, amen!

The old man is gone, *done away with,*

...<u>the new has come in Christ</u>!

So Paul says here in Philippians 3:7,

"But whatever <u>gain</u> I had,

...<u>I count it as loss</u>

...for the sake of Christ!

...Indeed I count <u>everything</u> as loss,

...<u>because of the surpassing worth</u>

...of <u>knowing Christ Jesus my Lord</u>."

He goes on to say:

"Hey Listen, **_For His sake I have suffered the loss of all things,_**

...**_and count them as refuse_** (<u>dung</u>)..."

Listen, don't miss this, there is a very important principle here:

Don't count what is lost _as a loss_,

...as something relevant and valuable that you have lost,

<u>Count it as refuse</u>,

...<u>as worth losing</u>,

...<u>as stinky refuse</u>,

...<u>as dung</u>, amen!

...for while you still count your past,

...your worldly wisdom,

...your old identity,

...your pride,

...as valuable,

...kind of plan B ...you know,

...in case God fails me,

...then you're in trouble already,

...you'll never be free from it!

No listen; don't see <u>any</u> value in it!

<u>Count it as refuse</u>!

Philippians 3:8

"...in order that I may gain Christ..."

Now how do I measure my gain in Christ?

Verse 9 says,

"<u>and be found in Him</u>..."

How?

By faith, not works!! Amen?

"<u>and be found in Him</u>..."

Discover yourself *in Him,* amen!

Discover *the truth about yourself* in Him!

Listen,

"Of God <u>are you</u> in Christ" - 1Corinthians 1:30

It has nothing to do with your own effort.

Romans 5:1

*"**Now we have peace with God** through our Lord Jesus Christ,"*

*"...**being justified by His Faith**..."*

2Corinthians 5:18 says,

*"**All <u>this is of God</u>,***

*...who through Christ (**through His death and resurrection**) reconciled us to himself"*

Philippians 3:9

*"...<u>**and be found in Him**</u>,*

...not having my own righteousness (a righteousness of my own making)*, based on the law* (based on works, my own achievements),

...but that (kind of righteousness) ***which is through faith in Christ,***

*...the righteousness that is **from God** and is of faith, **it is dependent on faith**,"*

(*It is **founded** on faith; it is **based on faith**, it comes **from faith**; it is **a direct result** of faith,*

*...it is a direct result of **insight and understanding**; revelation knowledge **into my identity in Him**,*

126

...my true original identity restored to me in Him,

...in His work of Redemption!

It is the exact opposite of fleshly pride).

Hallelujah!

You see the law of works will keep me confined to my own ability to achieve,

...while the law of faith links me to the achievement of God in Christ on my behalf.

The law of faith founds and secures me *upon His achievement,*

*...*it establishes me *in His achievement!*

It causes me to be grounded upon, and rooted *into His achievement!*

The law of faith <u>links me together</u> *with Him,*

*...*it grafts me in!

*...*I am grafted in, amen!

Hallelujah!

Chapter 7

Living a secure life

Let's also then take a look at Galatians.

I like the beginning of this epistle.

Paul says here in verse 1, and I quote to you from the *Ruach Translation*, he says,

Galatians 1:1

"I am not the product of man's schooling nor promoted by human organization, *but through Jesus Christ and God the Father who raised Him from the dead."*

Then he goes on to speak about the two kinds of gospels,

…the one that is related to Man's achievement

…and the other one;

*…***Christ's achievement.**

Then in verse 10 he says,

…out of the *Ruach Translation* again,

*"Am I now endeavoring to gain the favor of Man or God? Do I seek to please Man? I would not be a bond servant of Christ **if Man's applause would still persuade me.**"*

Do you see what the issue is here?

Man's gospel;

*…**the favor of Man; or the applause of Man related to Man's achievement,***

*…***or God's gospel;***

*…**the favor of God; or the applause of God related to <u>Christ's achievement</u>.***

What I want to draw your attention to is in chapter 3,

…and we're going to start reading in the *Ruach Translation* from verse 10,

…and I want you to note his strong language here,

He says,

Galatians 3:10

*"Those whose righteousness **is a product <u>of their keeping of the law</u> are under a curse**…"*

Listen, he is not talking about keeping the Law of Moses per se,

…because **although the Law <u>is done away with</u> in Christ, we are still fulfilling it, the core, the heart of it,** *the life portrayed there* in the Law of Moses;

…***the life*** the Law ***was only a shadow of; that life,***

…**as New Creations under the New Covenant, we are actually living** *that life!*

…*the Christ-Life!*

…*the Love-Life!*

…*the image and likeness of God!*

…*the Nature of God!*

…*that life we were originally designed to live!*

What he is talking about when he says that those who are keeping the law are under a curse, is not the Law of Moses per se,

…**but** *"the righteousness of works"*

He is talking about *"the law of works"* **people use as a basis to try and keep the Law of Moses.**

He says that they, *who employ "the law of works," and submit themselves under that system, and rule of life,*

"...are under a curse." - Galatians 3:10

"...for it is written:

'Cursed is everyone **who does not continue to <u>consistently</u> do every detail** of the Law!'

He is talking about *the inconsistency* in the righteousness dependent on works.

It is in itself a curse.

You see **if the blessing of God relates to** *life more abundantly*

What does the curse relate to?

An empty life, a life of lack, a life that is not abundant,

...an insecure life of inconsistency,

...a life of unfulfillment,

...a life of frustration.

Do you see that?

Do you see how my own efforts would <u>consistently frustrate me</u>?

God would not be pleased with that kind of a life for me!

Listen,

God does not want you to live a frustrated life, amen!

I do not believe God could be pleased with that.

God wants you to live a life at peace, amen!

…and God doesn't want to be robbed either of all the joys of an intimate relationship that is at peace.

All right, now where were we?

You see although the Law of Moses was holy, and just, and pure, and good, and of God,

*…*it was imperfect *and meant to be done away with.*

Why?

Because the problem with the Law of Moses is that it makes a demand upon an individual *who does not have the ability to keep it* …*outside of the knowledge of Christ,*

…outside of the righteousness <u>of faith</u>

The Law is **_OUTLINE_** the righteousness *of faith*.

You see **God only meant the Law <u>as a temporary measure</u>**

...until faith was revealed!

The Law was never meant to make Man righteous.

You see we cannot try to use the Law for something other than what it was meant for;

...for what it was not <u>designed</u> to be used for!

God had _a specific purpose_ in mind for the Law.

What was the purpose of the Law?

I indicated earlier that **the Law's purpose was to give Man the full knowledge of Sin, the knowledge of Sin's full measure, Sin's full extent.**

It reveals and exposes Sin to the fullest, <u>for what it really leaves us with</u>.

Why?

So I could see Sin, and sin, for what it is, *empty* and therefore detestable to me, *it steals kills and destroys;*

...I see it for what it really is, *so I'd want to be free from it!*

The purpose of the Law was *to prepare Man for* the good things *that were to come to us in Christ,*

...so Man would be ready for it,

...so he'd be hungry,

...starving for it,

...*so he'd want to welcome and embrace it, amen!*

The Law was merely, **a foretaste, <u>a shadow</u>** of *the good things to come to us in Christ.*

The Law **pointed toward;**

...it indicated *God's desire to define* <u>the quality of life</u>

...that He knew Man would be able to live,

...*once "the righteousness <u>that is of faith</u>" is revealed,*

...<u>*by which the power of Sin is broken*</u>.

So, **the Law provided a standard,**

…by which Man could measure his own efforts to justify himself,

…and so the Law actually revealed to man *the full extent of Sin's power over man,*

…and, therefore, *man's utter hopeless, miserable state under Sin's dominion!*

The Law *revealed and exposed Sin, and sin,* <u>**to the fullest**</u>,

…for what it really leaves us with!

At the same time the Law also awakened in Man *a longing after another kind of righteousness,* **other than his own,**

…a longing *to be justified APART FROM* **works,**

…a longing *to* again *be accepted;*

…to again be restored to innocence **before God,**

…<u>by God's own doing</u>,

…just like it was in the beginning when God first *brought Man forth out of Himself,*

…before the fall happened.

The Law awakened in Man a longing after *a righteousness _that is from God_,*

...in other words;

...*a righteousness **that is of faith**.*

So, to summarize again:

Do you see that *the Law did two things?*

- **The Law first of all *measured Sin's power and fruit* so that Man could be persuaded that his own efforts would just be one of hypocrisy and prideful deception if he would seek to find his righteousness in his own efforts.**

- The second thing was, and this is the most important thing about the Law: **the Law *began to awaken in Man a longing for righteousness by faith,***

    ...*a longing to again be accepted;*

    ...*a longing to again be restored in innocence before God,*

    ...**by God's own doing**.

Thus the end goal, the end purpose of the Law was *to be a shadow,*

...*to point us towards,*

…to give us a foretaste,

…to prepare us for,

…the kind of life we would only be able to live by revelation into the cross!

Thus the end goal, the end purpose of the Law was,

…to prepare us for,

…"righteousness by FAITH"

So, verse 11 of Galatians 3 says:

"It becomes evident then,

…that NO MAN WILL BE JUSTIFIED before God BY KEEPING THE LAW,

…but only he who THROUGH FAITH IS RIGHTEOUS will live."

"The Law does not operate by faith,

…but (the Law operates) by works."

Do you see those two laws here?

"…the law of faith"

Verses,

"…the law of works"

138

Galatians 3:12

"...for the one who keeps the Law will live by it..."

(In other words he will have to *"live by it,"*

...**he will have to** *"live by its requirements and consequences,"*

...**meaning** *he will be bound to operate by the law of works,*

...**he will remain in bondage to his own efforts,**

...**therefore he will remain under the curse,**

...*inconsistent, frustrated and unfulfilled*)

Then he writes about how,

Galatians 3:13

"Christ **redeemed us from** (bought us back out of the hands of) **the curse** *by becoming a curse* **on our behalf**...*"

According to the Vines Expository Dictionary of New Testament words, the verb *"redeem"* means **to exchange value, to buy out, or to release on receipt of ransom paid,** and it is usually used in reference to slavery, *in particular in reference to the release from slavery.*

I want you to know that when the Scripture says that,

"He redeemed us,"

…that means **it is a *legal* matter;**

…*it is a matter of law,*

He legally purchased *our release* from the curse,

…*our release* from slavery,

It was *a legal* transaction,

…and therefore *absolutely valid* and *vital* for the here and <u>now</u> of our experience!

That means *he introduced a new law*,

…<u>he brought us under *a new law*,</u>

…it means <u>the price He paid</u> *made our release legal!*

…*and valid* …*and REAL!*

We are no longer bound under an old law,

…but <u>*we are freed* by *a new law*,</u>

…*"the law of identification;"*

…*"the law of <u>faith</u>!"*

140

Chapter 8

Don't be put out

All right, let's also take a look at Galatians 5 quickly, and I'll read from verse 4 in the *Ruach Translation.*

Galatians 5:4

"Christ becomes <u>of no meaning</u> (of now value, of no practical benefit) *to you **since you seek God's approval by keeping the Law*** (or by subjecting yourself *to the law of works;* to the *curse* of that law; to the *consequences* of it; to the *inevitable fruit* of it);*"*

"YOU PUT YOURSELF <u>OUTSIDE</u> of the effect of His GRACE.*"*

When you subject yourself to the law of works;

…you put yourself outside of the effects of His grace!

…and then there is *nothing to draw upon* to bring about transformation

…there is *no power available* outside of the influence of grace!

In other words, <u>you ignore His approval He already gave you</u> in His GRACE towards you!

...<u>I will have to ignore His approval in unbelief,</u>

...and so actually INSULT what He did in Christ,

...*if I continue to try and add my works* to the completeness of His effort!

...then I am left outside in the dark and the cold again;

...there is *no power there in that place of double-mindedness,*

...there is *no power available* outside of the influence of *the TRUTH of redemption!*

...God can *only release grace and power* <u>based on faith in that truth!</u>

Listen, there's no substitute for *the law of <u>God's</u> applause.*

<u>FAITH</u> is *the law of <u>God's</u> applause.*

Hebrews 11:6

*"And **without faith it is impossible to please Him**..."*

Hey, even if the greatest patriarch of them all, father Abraham, could please Man through his own works, **he still doesn't stand approved before God,**

*...not until he became a man **who saw greater value in God's Word,** than in his own dreams and his own disappointments, and **he sided with the Word!***

I want you to notice that the moment **he *sided with the Word,***

*...**he began to make God's language his own**!*

It was FAITH, and *the law of FAITH* <u>that justified him,</u> *as he began to make God's language his own!*

*...**and as he *began to operate in that law of FAITH* <u>he began to enjoy a measure of LIFE</u> <u>that supersedes the kind of life any other law could give him</u>.***

I've heard Kenneth Copeland use a beautiful example of natural laws. He says that we all understand the law of gravity as a very consistent law; *what goes up must come down,* amen!

He says that **the only way that you can break through the law of gravity is through a law that *overrides* the law of gravity;** *it's called the law of lift,*

…otherwise you will never *become airborne,*

…and I'm talking about flying an aircraft here, not about the rapture ha… ha… ha…

You see **the law of lift causes me *to override* the law of pull and gravity**…

So when we discover **the law of faith**

…*the law of life* in Christ Jesus

…the *law of the Spirit*

…the *law of the mirror*

…the *law of identity*

…same law, amen!

…when we discover *that* law of lift;

…that *law of the Spirit*

…**that *comes into operation* through the hearing *that comes by the Word,***

…through **being in intimate relationship with God *through His Word,***

…through **waiting upon God,**

…*intertwining yourself with His word,*

*...intertwining yourself **with redemption realities,***

*...intertwining yourself **with His thoughts concerning you in Christ Jesus,***

*...intertwining yourself **with HIM!***

That law of liberty <u>comes into operation</u>,

...it <u>comes into operation</u> through *intimacy*, amen!

The Hebrew word for *"**waiting upon God**"* is: QAVAH.

To **wait upon the Lord**, to "QAVAH" means: -

To twist, to bind, to intertwine like a rope, to be strong and robust,

...from the idea of binding fast;

...it means **to become *intertwined*** with Him, to be ***intimately linked together*** with Him **in thought and language,**

...through *fellowship together **in the same TRUTH!***

It is called **intimate relationship!**

...*He* secures you, *He* anchors you, *He* becomes your foundation, that which you found yourself upon; your *strength,* your

source of life, the *stability* of your life, *the very force behind your life;*

...the very reason why you have life even when others don't!

So when I *discover myself* in the Word,

...when I discover myself *in Christ,*

...when I discover *the law of life* in Christ Jesus,

...the law of faith,

...the law of the Spirit,

...the law <u>that links me together</u> with God,

...with His Word and His Spirit,

...this law causes me <u>to soar</u> like an eagle,

...above yesterday's disappointments when I still ran on the ground and became weary and fell exhausted *in my own excellence,*

...exhausted *in my own energy...*

Mounting up with the wings of an eagle,

...<u>that's the life God has for us</u>!

Mounting up with *His* power,

...His energy, amen!

Hallelujah!

Praise the Lord!

I wanted to lay these truths as a foundation in your spirit through this book,

...and I hope I was able to communicate and lay that foundation real clearly,

...because I want you to begin from here and to have enough substance to help you further discover yourself in Christ!

Discover for yourself how the law of faith *works*,

*...*and **it *does* work**, amen!

I am telling you, *the law of faith works!*

It releases God's power within you,

...it releases an energy within you that will cause you to excel in your experience with God,

*...*above any boundary that you've ever found yourself locked in *through your own efforts.*

That's *the purpose* of faith, amen!

Faith is not just so that, you know, *you can believe to go to Heaven one day,* but **faith is *a law* of God,**

…**it's the <u>law</u> of *life,***

…**the <u>law</u> of the *Spirit*,**

…**it's the <u>law</u> of *liberty*,**

…***<u>it perfectly liberates</u>;***

…*it releases you to enjoy the quality of life God designed and desired for us to enjoy right from the beginning,*

…**the quality of life *that He has redeemed us for*,**

…**a life that satisfies Him *and fulfills us <u>to abundance</u>,* amen!**

Hallelujah!

I want you to go and explore these truths,

…**and I want you to allow these truths *to become so solid in your understanding*,**

…**that you will have no excuse,** .

…***you cannot help but* to live in the fruit of His travail,**

…*in the fruit of His labor,*

148

...in the fruit of His faith,

...entering into that rest of faith,

...that rest of *total fulfillment in faith,*

...that keeps you from your own labor!

It *keeps you,* amen!

...enjoying *the action of the Word,*

...activating you <u>from within</u>!

Hallelujah!

Praise the Lord!

Thank you Jesus!

Now, you don't need to read this next chapter *to enter in and fully enjoy what faith affords you* in your relationship with Father God and our Lord Jesus Christ,

...but I am including it anyway,

...to assist the few who might need a little help to get their faith activated,

...a kick-start if you will.

Chapter 9

Have faith from the heart

The Bible says in Romans 10:6-13

*"…the righteousness **BASED ON FAITH** (which is born of faith) **speaks this way**…"*

What does it say?

It says,

'**The Word is near you, <u>even in your mouth</u> and** (not just) **in your heart**'

What Word is he referring to?

He is not talking about the Bible; *he is talking about the Word that became flesh,*

…the word of Christ, the word concerning our redemption in Christ

"This then is also <u>THE WORD</u> OF FAITH which we preach"

*"…because **if <u>you</u> CONFESS <u>with YOUR mouth</u>**…"*

Not merely just saying that you believe it,

151

...**not only just believing it <u>in your head</u>,**

"...*but <u>actually</u> coming into agreement with God <u>within yourself, within your heart,</u>*

...*and then from your heart, <u>echoing your full agreement</u>*) ...*that Jesus <u>is</u> Lord...*"

Note: That Greek word used here for "*CONFESS*" is the word: HOMOLOGIA; from HOMOLOGEO which is made up of two words: HOMO – **the same** and LOGEO – **the written or spoken Word (the LOGOS)**.

In other words, it means: **to say the same**,

...and in this case **to come into *aggressive agreement* with the Word of God,**

...**or to *say the same thing as God says;***

...**to literally *echo your full agreement,***

...*about the **Lordship** of Jesus,*

...(about the pre-eminence of what God has revealed about Himself and about Man in Jesus, **the *ruler*-ship of these realities; the superiority of His sacrifice; <u>the success</u> of His accomplishment on that Cross)**...

...the *ruler*-ship of Jesus, His supremacy; He represents the fullness of time, the fullness of what could possibly be revealed in time concerning eternal realities! He represents the fullness of eternity! In Him the fullness of the Godhead dwelt in bodily form, and we are complete in Him; our completeness was also on display in Him. He represents both the fullness of God and the fullness of Man in one body!)

You see, you cannot really echo your full agreement *unless you actually believe these things,*

*...*unless *you actually believe* **that,**

*"...***He, who took on flesh and blood and became a man, and dwelt among us, had no other option but to represent Sin itself, and sin, in His flesh, so that, *in that sacrifice on that cross* you might become the righteousness of God**" – 2Corinthians 5:21

...so the word CONFESSION means:

*...***to come into aggressive agreement with God, *from the heart,* and therefore you also echo your agreement verbally, boldly,** about the Lordship of Jesus Christ (and His sacrifice) *and what it means; its implications in <u>your</u> life*...

...so when Paul uses the word CONFESSION here in this passage he actually means for you:

*...***to yield to it,**

*...***to receive it**

…in other words: **to believe it and to fully embrace it,**

 *…***to make it your own!**

You see; **we can only enjoy righteousness** *through Him,*

*…*through *yielding to Him,*

*…*through *coming into agreement with Him,*

*…*through coming into agreement *with what He did,*

*…*through <u>faith</u> *in His sacrifice,*

*…*through <u>believing</u> *in what He did,*

*…*through *actually yielding to Him!*

We can only enjoy righteousness through *our confession,*

…our confession **of faith**

…our **verbal, bold echo** *of these things* <u>**we have fully embraced**</u> **in our heart!**

We can only enjoy righteousness *through actually coming into agreement with His Word;*

*…***through actually believing it!**

In other words **you are not merely, <u>in a weak so-so agreement kind of a way</u> *saying the same thing as God says,***

...no, you are <u>echoing</u> the same thing as God,

...because it is <u>alive in your heart</u>;

...you are saying the same thing as God,

<u>...in full, verbal, bold, agreement</u>!

And you do not just believe *<u>in your head</u>,*

...you are not just merely <u>saying</u> the same thing as God,

'*...that Jesus conquered the power of sin and of the devil and was raised from the dead **because of my justification,***

...because He made me righteous again,

...because He restored my identity to me as child of God,

...and thereby restoring the image and likeness of God my Father <u>in me</u>'

...you are not just mouthing these things as a mere doctrine or teaching,

...you are not just saying these things and believing them in your head...

*...but **you see when you really do believe
these things,***

*...**you are actually** consenting to **that**
righteousness*,

*...**consenting to that identity,***

*...*consenting to that image and likeness of
your Father God in you,

*...and you are **coming into actual
agreement with God** about the Lordship of
Jesus Christ in your life,*

*...*joining yourself to His achievement,

*...*joining, linking, tying yourself to Him,

*...*to His righteousness,

*...*to His identity,

*...*to that image and likeness of the Father
on display in His life *...through faith*!

You are actually making *a real commitment
to YIELD TO* His Righteousness;

*...*and to the lordship of His *life*;

*...*to the *image and likeness* of Father God
on display in Him;

156

You are literally *making a real commitment* to *His Lordship* in your life!

So, Romans 10:9,

"...if you CONFESS with YOUR mouth that Jesus is Lord AND BELIEVE (while actually believing) in your heart that God raised Him from the dead (for your justification; because of your deliverance, because of your salvation, because of your righteousness,)"

"YOU WILL BE SAVED (you will be 'SOZO' in the Greek; you will be made whole)."

Let me say it again,

"IF YOU CONFESS WITH YOUR LIPS THAT JESUS IS LORD AND BELIEVE IN YOUR HEART THAT GOD RAISED HIM FROM THE DEAD (SO YOU CAN BE DELIVERED AND MADE WHOLE, THEN) YOU WILL BE SAVED (YOU WILL BE MADE WHOLE)."

"For a man believes in his heart (for real) and is justified (made righteous), and he confesses with his lips and so is (or gets, practically, in his experience) saved"

In other words *actually believing the truth* about your inclusion in Redemption and what it implies *will make you free,*

...just as Jesus said it would in John 8:32

The new King James Version of Romans 10:10 say:

"...you will be saved (delivered, rescued, made whole)*"*

"**because with the heart one believes <u>to</u> righteousness,**

(*...***one** *actually* **believes, or one believes <u>unto</u>, or one <u>believes ones way through to</u>** righteousness,

*...*one **believes <u>he is now</u> righteous,**

...his faith is credited to him or *reckoned **as** righteousness,*)

*... **<u>and with the mouth</u> confession is made <u>to</u> salvation,***

(Confession is made **about the reality of** salvation; or confession is made in order **<u>to get</u> <u>to</u> salvation, <u>to become</u> saved,** *to become* **whole;** or confession is made **<u>resulting in</u> salvation;**

*...***or confession is made** *fully embracing and echoing your full agreement, of what has already happened in the work of redemption*)

*"For the Scripture says, '***whoever** *BELIEVES* on Him (Jesus) **will not be put to shame***'*

(They will be victorious, they will be made whole, they will be saved; they will not be denied salvation!)

The RSV says,

"... **No one** *who* **BELIEVES** *in Him will be put to shame."*

Hallelujah!

Romans 10:13

"For ' everyone *(whoever, anyone; that means:* **EVERY SINGLE ONE**, *that includes me and* it includes *you*) *who* calls *upon (who fully identifies with) the name of the Lord* will be *(* shall be*) saved."*

1John 1:9 says:

"If we confess our sins"

(Note: Confessing your sins does not mean admitting to your sinful condition; *that you have been missing it in your life; that you have been missing out on the life He intended for you,*

...in other words *it is not a regret and remorse thing; it is not a guilt trip!*

*...*you may start there, **but then you have to move on** into the faith realm!

You have to also come into *aggressive, full, bold agreement with God,*

…*over your deliverance from* missing the mark, from sin, *through the sacrifice of Jesus Christ*)

…that is exactly then also what the word *"confess"* – HOMOLOGAO really mean:

TO COME INTO *FAITH-AGREEMENT* WITH GOD!

To agree with God on what?

It means **to agree with God <u>on the success of redemption</u>;**

…**that sin's hold over my life *was* and therefore *is* broken!**

See, **we are no longer justifying ourselves,**

…*no longer making excuses for missing the mark in our lives,*

…*because God's truth has awakened the desire within us to genuinely want sin out of our lives;*

…*to genuinely want to no longer miss the mark in our lives,*

…*and so faith and desire and passion and power have been awakened in us,*

...and we are employing it to get rid of that thing!

We are *echoing our total AMEN to redemption truth,*

...and so, we are coming into aggressive agreement with God in our hearts,

...but also verbally, **aggressively, passionately,**

...in total PERSUASION of the reality of what was done on that cross,

*...*so that *the actual power of God* can be *released* in our lives,

*...*and we can finally walk *free* from that lie and that deception and that lesser power;

*...*that inferior force of darkness trying to keep us bound!

The Scriptures go on to tell us what will happen then,

...it says,

1John 1:9

"He (God) is (then) faithful and just (based on what Jesus legally did for us *and based on the law of faith being activated and put into action by our faith-confession)"*

*"...**God is faithful and just to forgive us our sins** AND TO CLEANSE US (**to set us free from all missing the mark**) from all unrighteousness;*

(...**from anything that doesn't line up with righteousness; that doesn't line up with the image and likeness of Father God** *in us,* **with our** *true identity* **as child of God**)."

It says,

*"**He** will **forgive our sins** ...and cleanse us **(SET US FREE)** from all unrighteousness,"*

The word *"to cleanse"* is used in our everyday language to indicate **the removal of foreign matter,**

...the removal of something **that does not belong!**

Hallelujah!

Listen, **it can start happening to you;**

...**you can start experiencing it** in a practical way **in your life,** with just a simple prayer of faith!

If you pray a prayer from your heart **...especially if you pray** because you believe,

God hears every word,

162

...because He is not far from any one of us;

He <u>will</u> answer your prayer,

...and I guarantee you things between you and He will never be the same again,

...I mean in a good way;

...things between you and Him will be made totally new and beautiful!

He wants to draw you into intimate fellowship with Himself,

...because you already are His own dear child, because He loves you!

He wants you to return to *where you belong;*

...the family and household of your very own Daddy God!

He wants to set you free from the power sin has over your life,

...and as you really believe the truth of His word, the truth of redemption, He <u>will</u> help you defeat sin and drive it out of your life!

He <u>will</u> fill you with His love; with Himself *if you want Him to!*

He wants to <u>activate</u> *your true design; His nature; His love <u>within you</u>;*

...that true image and likeness in which you have been made,

...so you may live life the way God designed it to be lived!

You are welcome to pray this now from your heart if you so choose:

Lord Jesus, thank you for dying for my sin on the cross *that I may be set free!*

Father God, thank you for forgiving my sin *and blotting it out on that cross.*

Thank you *for accepting me back into your family.*

Thank you *for blameless, innocent fellowship with You!*

Father, right now *I embrace the gift of righteousness.*

Jesus, You are the Christ, *be Lord in my life.*

I yield *my whole being* to You now; *I invite You in!*

Lord Jesus open my spiritual eyes and ears *to all that You have for me*;

164

Do it Lord, I ask, do it *by Your Word and by Your Spirit.*

I do believe the TRUTH of what You accomplished FOR ME in Your work of redemption!

Thank you for *changing me from the inside out.*

Amen!

Amen means: **let it be to me** *according to Your Word! Your Word is Truth! I echo my full agreement with YOU, with YOUR WORD! Therefore let it be, and I believe it will <u>BE</u> just as I have prayed.*

Now, if you received your righteousness and salvation **by faith;**

…*by believing in the success of Jesus' sacrifice; and by believing that God heard you,* you probably already feel different, *because you connected with God in a real way, believing the truth, and committing yourself in a real way to relationship with God,*

…**but even if you feel nothing it cannot change THE TRUTH!**

The REALITY is that God heard you, *and His power is at work in you <u>even now</u>*!

The Scripture says in 1Corinthians 6:17 that,

*"He who is joined to the Lord **is one spirit with Him**…"*

It also says in 2Corinthians 5:17 that

*"If anyone is in Christ, **he is a new creation**, the old things* (what was true about your life, the old realities, your old righteousness, your old mindset, your old belief-system) **have pass**ed **away, behold all things have become new**."*

If you want to grow in intimate relationship and friendship with God,

*…then the Word of God; the Truth of God; Redemption Realities; What Father God has to say to us and about our new identity in Jesus Christ **must continue to find a genuine place of honor and respect and agreement, it must find its rightful place in your heart**.*

The apostle Peter said in 1Peter 2:2 & 3 that

"…like newborn infants, (you must passionately crave after) **earnestly desire**, *the* (**pure** spiritual) *milk*; (**the TRUTH**) *of the Word **that you may grow thereby**…"*

"…if indeed you have tasted that the Lord is good"

God has been real with you; His love is real, and if He is now real to you, *then be real with God;*

...don't pretend, don't be fake, and don't play games with Him!

...after all, God sees right through all of it!

God means business with you, *so mean business with God!*

I mean, *mean business with His Word!*

What I am trying to say is:

If Jesus Christ truly is now Your LORD,

...then be sure to treasure; to believe and embrace; to live by the truths concerning your redemption;

...that means the real truths concerning you, revealed in the Word; in Christ!

Read about Jesus in Matthew, Mark, Luke and John

...and believe in Him;

...believe that He is indeed the mirror of your life;

...that He is the kind of person and that He lived that kind of life full of love and full of

God that *you were originally designed for and are now restored to live*.

However He lived His life;

…*the kind of love and faith He walked in,*

…*the quality of relationship with God He enjoyed as Daddy and friend,*

…*and whatever He was able to do because of walking in that kind of love and faith and friendship with God,*

…and also whatever He told His disciples they could and should be able to do *by that same faith and love, and friendship with God as Father,*

…*you can and should live your life that way to;*

…*you can do those things too!*

It's for you too;

…it's relevant for today!

It's your inheritance as a child of God!

Read also the book of Acts and the letters of the apostles to the churches.

Treasure what He has to say in His Word in your heart.

BELIEVE IT and live your life consistently by it, <u>not just when you feel like you can agree with it</u>.

YIELD YOURSELF TO GOD!

Walk in the God kind of love!

Walk in *His* image and likeness!

Walk in that image and likeness *you were made in!*

...you were made in *His* image and likeness!

<u>God is love</u>!

And so are <u>you</u>!

Live that kind of life!

Those letters to the churches the apostles wrote, was not just written to those people back then, but to us as well, because we are also part of the Church and need to receive from those Scriptures, *"...reproof, correction, and instruction **in righteousness**."*

In John 17 Jesus prayed for us and this is what He prayed:

John 17:1

"Father, the hour has come. Glorify Your Son, that Your Son also may glorify You,

…as You have given Him authority over all flesh, **that He should give eternal life** *to the many You have given Him."*

(That means *everyone who believes,* that means all of us, <u>you</u> included! Amen!)

*"***<u>And this is eternal life</u>, that they may KNOW** (fully know, intimately know) **You, the only true God, and Jesus Christ whom You have sent.***"*

It's all about developing <u>a real relationship</u> with God <u>by believing His Word</u>.

John 17:6

"I have manifested Your name to these (those who have received Him and believe Him) *whom You have given Me out of the world.* **They were Yours,** *You gave them to Me…"*

How did God give us to Jesus?

It was by the power of His Word and the power of the Holy Spirit to persuade us in the truth.

He drew us *by His Spirit.*

He attracted us *to the life that is in Jesus…*

170

...He persuaded us and convinced us and saved us *through the truth and power of His Word!*

John 17:6

"They were Yours, You gave them to Me, and they have kept Your Word."

How have we kept His Word?

By believing it, treasuring it, embracing it *as reality;*

...by echoing *our full agreement* and by *living it and being it!*

...by *yielding to it,* and allowing it to work *in us,*

...allowing it to be rooted and grounded in the soil of our hearts *and affect our thinking and our person, and our behavior,*

...allowing it *to shape and mold our belief-system and our very lives;*

...and allowing it to become *our lifestyle,*

...allowing it to become us, *our very life!*

John 17:8

"For I have given them the words which You have given Me; and <u>they have received</u>

them *…they believed them, treasured them and embraced them and held fast to them…"*

That's how the Father gave us to Jesus and how we became His disciples.

John 17:16

*"**They are not of the world,***

(and no longer live by the standards of worldly thinking and worldly wisdom)

*…**just as I am not of the world**"*

*"**Set them apart…**"*

(Cleanse them, set them free from ignorance, from the influence of darkness, from the influence of confusion and missing the mark, from the influence of the world and worldly wisdom, *and draw them closer to yourself*)

*"…**by YOUR Truth; YOUR WORD IS TRUTH.**"*

He also said this in John 14, 15, 16:

John 14:23

*"If anyone loves Me, **he will keep** (believe, treasure, embrace, hold fast to, live by) **My Word** (by the truth of redemption);*

172

"And My Father will love him, and We will come to him, and make our home with him."

John 15:9

"__Just as the Father has loved Me, I have also loved you__; abide in My love."

John 15 verse 4 says,

"Abide in Me …and Me in you."

How?

By believing and treasuring His Word (His redemption truth).

John 15:4

*"As the branch cannot bear fruit of itself, **unless it abides** in the vine,*

*…so **neither can you, __unless you abide in Me__.**"*

"I am the vine, you are the branches;

*…**He who abides in Me, and I in him, he bears much fruit;**"*

*"**By this My Father is glorified, that you bear much fruit;***

…and by this fruit you bear it will be apparent that you are My disciples."

John 15:14

"You are my friends if you <u>do</u> whatever I command you,

(…**in other words, if you believe and fully embrace these truths I have shared with you *as reality*).**"

John 15:10

"If you <u>keep</u> (believe, treasure, embrace and live the things I have spoken to you) *my commandments* **(the things I have shared with you as reality and commanded you to believe concerning what is accomplished in redemption),**

…**then,**

" <u>**you will abide in My love,**</u> *just as I have kept* (believed, treasured, embraced and lived) *My Father's commandments* **(the truth He has revealed to me as reality and commanded me to believe about the incarnation and what is to be accomplished in redemption),** *and abide in His love."*

"This is My commandment, <u>that you love one another just as I have loved you</u>."

(That life of love is the only authentic life you can live! It's the life of your design!

...there is no true fulfillment outside of living that kind of love; living that kind of life!)

"This I command you, that you love one another"

(That is what life and ultimate reality is all about: LOVE)

Jesus commanded us *to love everyone;*

...all people, no matter how different they are from us, no matter what culture or race,

...but especially other Christian brothers and sisters

In another place He made it clear that He meant *everyone* when He said,

"Love your enemies..." - Matthew 5:44

...that means people you can't get along with at all,

...or that can't get along with you at all,

...it means people you may have hated for any reason, or that may still hate you for whatever reason.

Remember you already are a new creation NOW *and therefore you are well able to do this.*

You were created for it.

You were created *and set free* <u>to give full expression to your Father's image and likeness</u>; *to His love nature!*

After all *He is your real Father who gave your spirit birth!*

...He is the One who formed you and fashioned you and then placed *you* in your mother's womb,

...*and there he clothed <u>you</u> with flesh,*

...He merely *clothed you* with flesh,

...but *you* <u>are more</u> than flesh and blood.

You may live in a flesh and blood body,

...<u>but you are a spirit being,</u>

...<u>made in the image and likeness of God</u>,

...*and through faith <u>you have now been released to live the life you were always designed for</u> right from the very beginning.*

God your Father will most certainly strengthen you *by His Spirit within you* and help you *live in this <u>reality</u>,*

...He will assist you with loving *even* your enemies.

If you ask Him, He will lead you and help you get connected in fellowship with other Christians *who believe and live by* this new kind of righteousness and preach these new creation *realities.*

Ask Him to connect you with Christians *that is totally filled with the Holy Spirit and can speak in other tongues just like the believers in the book of Acts.*

They will share with you, and help you get totally filled in the Holy Spirit yourself too,

...or you can contact me and I will help you, *but you really need to connect with a body of believers there locally where you live.*

They will love you and be there for you *as <u>true</u> family,*

...because, in fact, *we <u>are</u> family,*

...and they will encourage you as you grow spiritually in this new kind of righteousness.

I cannot emphasize enough how important it is for you to be part of a local body of believers,

...and for you to have someone who has been totally filled with the Holy Spirit and speaks in other tongues to *lay hands on you so that you may also be immersed in the same power of the Holy Spirit that is in them.*

This transference of power is very important, *because you need to be endued with the power of the Holy Spirit,* so the light that shines out from you as a Christian in the midst of a crooked and perverse world *may be even stronger and brighter and full of power and anointing;*

...the real purpose of it all is *so that you can be a better witness for the Lord Jesus Christ;*

...*bearing witness to the reality of redemption, with the power of the Holy Spirit, and with signs and wonders and healings and miracles following your witness.*

I also cannot emphasize enough how important it is for you to develop <u>real</u> relationships *with other genuine Christians,*

...<u>in order for you to become a part of</u> the extended family of God *<u>in a real, genuine, and practical way</u>!*

Satan is always trying *to cause division* through the breakdown *of <u>genuine</u> relationships.*

If he can get you *unattached and isolated,* then he can stunt your growth *and keep you from making progress in the things of God.*

Remember this:

"...two is better than one and a threefold cord is not easily broken."

In fact I am quoting from Ecclesiastes 4:9-12 which says,

"Two are better than one, (1) because they have a good reward for their labour. (2) For if they fall, one will lift up his companion"

"But woe to him who is alone when he falls,

...for he has no one to help him up"

"Again, if two lie down together, (3) they will keep warm;

...but how can one be warm alone?"

"Though (4) one may be overpowered by another, two can withstand him.

And (three is even better than two) a threefold cord is not quickly broken."

Jesus said that the world would come to know Him by the love we have for one another.

It is His desire for us to walk *in genuine fellowship with one another,*

…and <u>together</u>,

"*…have good reward for our labour;*"

…in other words,

He wants us, <u>*TOGETHER*</u>, to make *a real spiritual and practical difference* in this world we live in,

…bringing into reconciliation with Father God a harvest of souls;

…that is what glorifying King Jesus is all about.

We are to love people in such a pure and powerful way that we set them free from the sin that is destroying their lives,

…and do everything we can *to rescue them with the truth of the Word; <u>with the TRUTH of THEIR redemption</u>!*

In closing, I urge you to get yourself a copy of *"The Mirror Bible"* available online at: <u>www.friendsofthemirror.com</u> or at <u>www.amazon.com</u> and several other book sellers.

If you want me or someone a part of our team to come to where you are, *anywhere in the world,* and give a talk or teach you and some of your friends *about the gospel message,* simply contact us at www.livingwordintl.com …or you can always find me on www.facebook.com

I pray that God may richly bless you in your life and that you would prosper and be in health even as your soul prospers in enjoying *a righteousness that is **of** faith* as you begin to enter into this new kind of relationship with God which **He** has brought you into.

If your life has changed as a result of reading this book, please write to me and let me know.

I would love to share your joy,

…so that my joy in writing this book *may be full!*

"That which was
from the beginning,

which we have heard
(not just with our natural ears but
with our spiritual ears),

which we have seen with our eyes
(not just our natural eyes
but **our spiritual eyes)**,

which we have looked upon
**(beheld, focused our attention
upon)**,

and our hands have handled

(not just our natural hands but **our spiritual hands have also handled,**

or you could say:

which we have also spiritually experienced,
or experienced in our spirit,
in our inner man of the heart),

concerning <u>the Word of life</u> –

that which we have seen and heard
(not just in the natural but
in our spirit by the Spirit of God)

we declare (and make known) to
you,

so you also may have (this)
fellowship with us;

and truly our fellowship is with the
Father and with His Son Jesus
Christ.

And these things we write to you

That your joy
may be full!"

– 1 John 1:1, 3 and 4

185

About the author

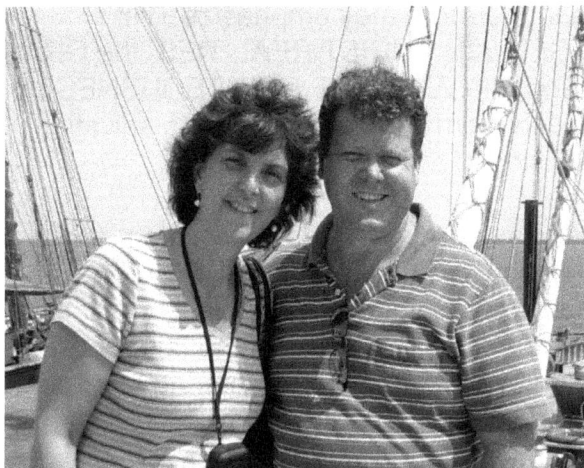

Rudi & Carmen Louw together oversee and pastor a church: Living Word International. They also travel and minister both locally and internationally.

Rudi was born and raised in the country of South Africa, while Carmen grew up in Cortland, New York.

They function in the ministry of reconciliation (2Corinthians 5:18-21) and flow strongly in the gifts of the Holy Spirit and His anointing to teach, preach, prophecy, heal and whatever is needed to touch people's lives with the reality of God's love and power.

God has given them keen insight into what He has to say to mankind in the work of redemption, concerning the revelation of, and restoration of, humanity's true identity,

…and therefore they emphasize THE GOSPEL; IN CHRIST REALITIES; the GRACE of God; the WORD OF RIGHTEOUSNESS and all such eternal truths essential to salvation and living of the CHRIST-LIFE.

They have been granted this wisdom and revelation into the knowledge of God by the resurrected Spirit of Jesus Christ, to establish and strengthen believers in the faith of God, and to activate them in ministering to others.

Not only are people set free from the poison and bondage of sin, condemnation and all kinds of intimidation, (upheld, strengthened and reinforced by age old religious ideas born out of ignorance,) but many are brought into a closer more intimate relationship with Father God, as Daddy, through accurate teaching, and unveiling of the gospel message, prophetic words, healings and miracles.

Rudi & Carmen are closely knitted together with many other effective Christians, church fellowships, and groups of believers who share the same revelation and passion.